Tweet If You

 **Jesus**

Practicing Church
in the Digital
Reformation

More Advance Praise for *Tweet If You* ♥ *Jesus*

Our churches are in an incredible time of transition, and it seems like mainline churches prefer to pretend it's 1957, not 2011. We are quickly falling behind not only the wider culture, but non-denominational churches that recognize that we have to adapt to thrive. This book will help your church move into the future, which is where we're all headed anyway.

—The Rev. N. Graham Standish, author of *In God's Presence: Encountering, Experiencing, and Embracing the Holy in Worship* and pastor of Calvin Presbyterian Church (Pittsburgh area)

A self-proclaimed "digital optimist," Elizabeth Drescher masterfully contextualizes digital media and social networking in the history of human communications and faithful people's practices of listening, attending, connecting, and engaging with one another and our deepest traditions. Deftly weaving stories of how church leaders are using these emerging technologies, she connects social analysis and theology to provide a map for those feeling lost in the "Digital Reformation."

—Julie A. Lytle, Associate Professor and Director of EDS Connect: Resources for Theology and Practice at Episcopal Divinity School (Cambridge, Massachusetts)

Elizabeth Drescher makes crucial and life-giving connections between the practices of the desert fathers and mothers, and the digital social media reformation we're inhabiting at the moment. Like Parker Palmer and Clay Shirky, Drescher shares stories of our relational practice with a clarity and vividness that draws you into her hopeful—but still critical—engagement with the digital social media reformation currently underway. This book will be a required text in my courses!

—Mary Hess, Associate Professor of Educational Leadership at Luther Seminary (St. Paul, Minnesota)

In *Tweet If You* ♥ *Jesus*, Elizabeth Drescher presents social media as a natural extension of our long history of communicating and leading in ways that uniquely suit our times. She proposes the startling idea of leadership as place, inviting us to create spaces in which we can "lead with compassionate welcome." Drescher opens a door to understanding social media; those of us who step through will find inspiration and refreshing insights to inform our practice of leadership and communication.

—Patricia Beck Carr, author of *Implementing Culture Change* and Assistant Professor of Organizational Learning & Leadership at Gannon University (Erie, Pennsylvania)

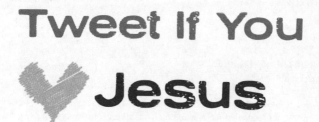

Tweet If You ♥ Jesus

Practicing Church in the Digital Reformation

Elizabeth Drescher

Morehouse Publishing
NEW YORK · HARRISBURG · DENVER

Unless otherwise indicated, all passages from the scriptures are from the *New Revised Standard Version* of the Bible © 1989 by the Division of Christian Education of the National Council of Churches of Christ in the U.S.A. Used by permission. All rights reserved.

Excerpt from "Little Gidding" text by T. S. Eliot © 1943 by T.S. Eliot, © renewed 1971 by Esme Valerie Eliot. Harcourt Books. Used by permission.

Library of Congress Cataloging-in-Publication Data

Drescher, Elizabeth.
    Tweet if you [heart] Jesus : practicing church in the digital reformation / Elizabeth Drescher.
        p. cm.
    On t.p. "[heart]" appears as a heart.
    Includes bibliographical references.
    ISBN 978-0-8192-2423-1 (pbk.)—ISBN 978-0-8192-2452-1 (e-book) 1. Internet in church work. 2. Social media and religion. 3. Church work—Protestant churches. I. Title.
    BR99.74.D74 2011
    253.0285'675—dc22
                                        2011002389

Cover design by Laurie Klein Westhafer.
Illustrations © 2010 by Angelo Lopez. Used by permission.

Printed in the United States of America.

Morehouse Publishing, 4775 Linglestown Road, Harrisburg, PA 17112
Morehouse Publishing, 445 Fifth Avenue, New York, New York 10016
Morehouse Publishing is an imprint of Church Publishing Incorporated.
www.churchpublishing.org

For Kelly Simons

Contents

Acknowledgments

The writing of *Tweet If You ♥ Jesus* has benefited from much digital sociality, perhaps most notably among a number of leaders in digital ministry highlighted throughout whom I know only by way of digital social media connections and communities: Keith Anderson, Andy Doyle, Ryan Dry, Ron Pogue, Susan Russell, Ruth VanDemark, and Chris Yaw. These generous digital colleagues were joined by others I do know from face-to-face engagements: Diane Bowers, Greta Huls, Walter Knowles, Bruce Robison, and Kirk Smith. I am grateful to all of these friends and colleagues for their willingness to share precious time and valuable insights that have brought life to this book. I am likewise grateful to Steven Bauman, Greg Troxell, Janet Fouts, Steve Dueck, and David Buehler for regularly sharing resources that enriched my understanding of the technical, cultural, and ecclesial change I attempt to describe in the book.

Jerry Campbell of Church Divinity School of the Pacific prompted the thinking that led to this project by inviting me to speak on the topic of social media and the Church in the Episcopal Diocese of Arizona and at St. Mark's Cathedral in Seattle. Lisa Webster gave me the opportunity to explore many of the ideas I develop more fully this book in the online magazine *Religion Dispatches*. My deepest thanks to Lisa and Evan Derkacz for inviting me into such an amazing community of scholars and writers on contemporary religion. Likewise, Carin Jacobs of the Center for the Arts, Religion & Education invited me to speak on social media and religion, which prompted me to further consider connections between contemporary and medieval practices of communication and community. A grant from the Wabash Center for Teaching & Learning in Religion & Theology with Kris Veldheer of the Graduate Theological Union library enabled me to explore the evolution of learning practices in relation to social media. Finally, a paper presented at the 2010 Annual Meeting of the American Academy of Religion gave me the chance to fine tune my thinking on digital leadership in ministry with an energetic gathering of colleagues.

These engagements provided invaluable opportunities to enter the ideas presented here into challenging and enriching conversations with a diverse community of ministers, scholars, and writers.

Two people have been especially involved in the completion of *Tweet if You ♥ Jesus*. Angelo Lopez, whose cartoons I first encountered through the Episcopal Diocese of El Camino Real Facebook page, provided the illustrations throughout the book. This means that Angelo was among the very first readers of the book, and I so appreciate having had the opportunity to see very early drafts through his eyes. Stephanie Spellers, my remarkably gifted editor, by far surpassed the editorial cliché of being a sensitive and sharp-eyed reader whose attention to my writing made for a much better book than would otherwise have been possible. Her practical wisdom, organizational skills, and kind but firm insistence that I step away from various rabbit holes has made for a much more accessible book than I could possibly have written on my own. Nevertheless, it goes almost without saying that all of the shortcomings in what follows are mine alone.

Many thanks also to Patrick Malloy, who introduced me to Frank Tedeschi at Church Publishing, setting in motion the publication of this book. I am grateful to Frank for his enthusiasm for the project from the earliest days. Likewise, I am deeply appreciative to everyone at Church Publishing/Morehouse for taking this book seriously and for giving the project so much support.

Lastly, I suppose some of my interest in digital social media comes from a lifetime of having been blessed with a kind and generous network of geographically distributed friends, most of whom I am now much more able to stay in touch with because of Facebook and Twitter. All of these friends have been sources of encouragement during the writing of this book, but I would particularly like to thank Alyssa Ninan Nickell, Steven Bauman, Cheryl DeGrasse, Donna Freitas, Aimee Wright Lowe, Andrew Lowe, Maureen Beyer Moser, Cathy Powell, Wanda Guthrie, Matt Fisher, and Ellen McGrath Smith for the many perfectly timed shout-outs that made the writing of this book so much easier.

Elizabeth Drescher, PhD
San Jose, California
Feast of the Epiphany, 2011

SIGNS & WONDERS

Appropriately enough, this book began as an extended conversation across diverse communities spanning a wide geographical area. It did not, however, begin online. Rather, it started in old-school fashion, through a series of talks I was invited to deliver by Jerry Campbell, the vice president of advancement at Church Divinity School of the Pacific, an Episcopal seminary in Berkeley, California. At the time, I was the director of a continuing education center with a well-established online learning program in need of some digital updating. In the midst of my efforts to nudge the program away from the dial-up culture that had defined its first decade to the digital reality that was rapidly leaving it behind, Jerry asked me if I would deliver a talk to a couple groups of CDSP alums and supporters in the Episcopal Diocese of Arizona.

My charge was to discuss "whatever you're passionate about," which at that moment was the challenge of engaging members of a predominantly fiftysomething mainline Protestant denomination in more accessible, flexible, and affordable modes of learning. So I decided to put together a talk on something I was really just beginning to grasp myself: the cultural transformation associated with new digital social media as it impacted religious practice. My hope was that the twenty or thirty people Jerry suggested might turn up for these talks would offer some feedback on my early research on the topic and provide insight into the day-to-day relationship between technology and religion in a small, but still influential, mainline Protestant denomination.

I had found in my initial explorations, unsurprisingly, that Evangelical and non-denominational churches had embraced a certain version of digital communication that extended from church community to theological education and formation. The online Evangelical ministry portal Streaming Faith, for instance, uses slick, state-of-the-art media to minister to more than a million site visitors every month. Pat Robertson's Regent University offers an extensive, accredited online learning program with degree options from undergraduate to doctoral levels across the liberal arts, including religion and theology. Non-denominational megachurches like Seattle's Mars Hill Church and Chicago's Harvest Bible Chapel sport Java-swank websites where ministry and religious education are offered up in attractive morsels that mark a path for believers and seekers to follow into face-to-face church community. Videos, podcasts, blogs, interactive social media hubs, Facebook and Twitter links with regular feeds from pastors and educators, and (of course) easy online donation portals characterize the web presence of the fastest-growing Christian communities in the United States and across the globe.

But what of Episcopal, Lutheran, Methodist, and Presbyterian (or Roman Catholic, for that matter) digital practice for ministry? Before a "Tweet If You ♥ Jesus" talk in Phoenix, The Right Reverend Kirk Smith, bishop of the Episcopal Diocese of Arizona and a historian by academic training, offered up a succinct summary of both the history of the mainline churches' engagement with new media and the challenge faced today. "Well," he said, "we blew it with radio; we blew it with television. The question is whether we'll be able to make use of these new tools while there is still a window of opportunity."

Characteristically dowdy church web pages and lingering social media phobia notwithstanding, what grew to be a series of talks through 2009 and early 2010 made clear to me that mainline Protestants are ready to open the digital window more than a crack. The first talks in Tucson and Phoenix, to significantly more than the twenty to thirty attendees anticipated, led to further talks in

Seattle, Berkeley, and at the General Convention of the Episcopal Church in Anaheim in 2009. That prompted more talks to gatherings of clergy and laity across the age spectrum in the Episcopal Diocese of El Camino Real in Salinas, California, and with denominationally mixed groups of clergy and lay leaders in Chicago and in Mountain View, California.

While I might like to think that attendance at these talks had to do with my dynamic presentation style and novel command of the material, alas, no one who came really knew who I was. What they knew was that their churches were struggling, and they suspected that at least some of this was related to the exponential growth of the internet and, in particular, to things like texting on smartphones, tweeting on Twitter, and posting on Facebook. They also seemed to get that the changes their churches and other ministries were experiencing would not be addressed by simply updating their websites, starting a blog, or running a Twitter feed.

Over the course of the year, these face-to-face conversations with hundreds of ministry leaders brought home the point that the Church is at a critical juncture as it attempts to respond to dramatic cultural changes related to new mobile, digital social media. Some of those changes are wonderfully liberating, inviting creative involvement in the practice of faith and the nurturing of community by believers and seekers of all stripes around the globe. Others, such as the restructuring of concepts of privacy, self-presentation, and relationship that seem to undermine notions of interpersonal, communal, and spiritual intimacy at the heart of much Christian practice, feel more troubling. Threatening, even.

What I heard over and over was that people in mainline churches did not understand digital technologies on a functional level and had not begun to fully grasp their cultural impact. But unfamiliar though these new technologies were to many people, it was the nature of social exchange and cultural engagement emerging from broad adoption of new social digital media that felt so alien and alienating. Sure, people needed how-to advice on setting up a Facebook group or developing a Twitter feed. But the sort of question I heard again and again about Twitter and Facebook participation—*"But why would anyone want to know what I had for breakfast?"*—is not a technical, how-to question. It stands for a much deeper social question of the sort that lies at the root of the anxiety that many people feel over new digital media in general and especially in the deeply social contexts of religious practice. *Who is the 'me' I present when people I usually only see on Sunday, and then only really engage for a short time over coffee, see photos of my trip to Patagonia, my dog, and my nephew's wedding? How is the nature of our relationship changed by this digitally mediated engagement? How does this new unfolding of our relationship enter into our established, face-to-face community?* Such questions speak to the mix of concern and possibility about changing social realities that are at the center of our current preoccupation with digital social media and associated mobile computing.

The people I met brought what amounted to complex theological questions to their exploration of digital media. They were uncertain about what resources, if any, were available within the Christian tradition to meaningfully address these questions. *What does it mean to "love your neighbor" in a world in which a "friend" might as easily be the kid from down the street you grew up with as a woman in Botswana whom you've never seen in person and only know in the context of Facebook status updates, photos, and notes? What is the nature of a community at prayer in a compline service tweeted each evening by the cybermonks of Virtual Abbey? What is the ecclesiological and liturgical significance of worship in the various churches across the theological spectrum on the quasi-3D, virtual reality site "Second Life"? How can we negotiate spiritual interaction in these new contexts without losing sight of basic elements of Christian faith expressed in traditional embodied and geographically located practices of prayer, worship, and compassion toward others?*

Beyond this, The Very Reverend David Bird, Ph.D., dean of Trinity Episcopal Cathedral in San Jose, California, added a nuts-and-bolts question about social media engagement to the list at a "Tweet If You ♥ Jesus" presentation in Berkeley: *What obligations are created—spiritual, moral, and legal—when a visitor to a church's or other religious group's website or Facebook page appears to be in crisis or danger?* While Bird's question has pastoral and legal implications that are well beyond the scope of this book to address, it nonetheless highlights the significance of the cultural transition in which we currently find ourselves as it applies to every aspect of the Church.

Pilgrims, Skeptics & Pioneers: The Audience for this Book

This book is for people who are asking all of these sorts of questions. It is for people committed to a wide range of lay and ordained, formal and informal ministries in the Church, and who understand that such ministries necessarily feel the impact of any new, expansive social and cultural change. These leaders in ministry see the signs of this change all around them—a transformation that I argue amounts to nothing less than a full-on Digital Reformation—but they are not quite sure how to meaningfully integrate new digital social media into the practice of ministry. In the pages ahead, such readers will find an exploration of the way digital social media are changing practices of communication, community, and leadership and how, at the same time, they are reconnecting us to ancient and medieval relational practices that have been forgotten or abandoned in the centuries since the European Reformations. It is my hope that *Tweet If You ♥ Jesus* will provide resources that help pilgrims of the Digital Reformation to engage social media with greater creativity and confidence.

Tweet If You ♥ Jesus is also a book for digital social media skeptics, including those who see no place for trendy, brain-rotting nonsense such as Facebook and Twitter in the life of the Church. They, too, see the signs of change related to social media everywhere, but they wonder if we ought to spend our time, attention, and other limited resources in a media landscape that presents tremendous risks right alongside unexplored possibilities. My hope is that the chapters ahead will reassure faithful critics that new media hold much promise for mainline churches precisely because they are based on ways of communicating, leading, and nurturing community that, unlike the broadcast media that largely passed mainline churches by, echo the best of our history and traditions. While such reassurances may not set pessimists in the Digital Reformation a-tweeting with wild abandon, my hope is that this book will at least enable them to better understand, and perhaps even appreciate, why so many in their communities are anxious to take up new (and, as we shall see, renewed) practices of church in diverse social media locales.

Finally, *Tweet If You ♥ Jesus* is written for the many leaders in ministry who are already actively and creatively participating in social media communities by way of extending and enriching their service to the Church in the world. As the pages ahead will make clear, I have learned much from these digital pioneers in ministry. Even as I discuss some of the practices of digital ministry they have undertaken, I offer this book as an invitation to continue to share resources and practices, and to collaborate within and across church communities. In that light, although this book is now finished, I hope that it is only the beginning of an extended conversation about what it means to be the Church in the early days of the Digital Reformation.

WELCOME TO THE DIGITAL REFORMATION

I am about to do a new thing; now it springs forth, do you not perceive it?

—*Isaiah 43:19*

For people engaged in the life of the Church, whether as believers, seekers, or observers, the cultural changes associated with new digital social media practices mark the early stages of a reformation of the Church—a *Digital Reformation*. This reformation is not entirely about digital technologies and their effect on human consciousness, relatedness, and communication. It's also driven by economic, environmental, political, intellectual, and a whole host of other issues that have been reconfigured at an increasingly rapid pace since the end of World War II, as the period of modernity that shaped the last great religious enlightenment reached its zenith and began to wane. However, the recent ascendency of digital technologies—particularly digital social media such as Facebook, Twitter, and YouTube—functions as an animated symbol of radical new globalized modes of access, participation, co-creativity, and distributed authority to an extent that makes clear that any reshaping or (we hope) revitalizing of the Church will largely be defined in relationship to the digital milieu.

Like the reformations of the twelfth and sixteenth centuries, the Digital Reformation has some revolutionary elements, but it is not about replacing one form of religious practice with another, in the way that eighteenth-century political revolutionaries in France and America sought to replace monarchy with democracy. Rather, the Digital Reformation has in common with earlier projects of reform the impulse to reclaim something of the spiritual practices of early church communities for believers today. Where the Digital Reformation is different, however, is that it is more plainly driven by the often ad hoc spiritualities of ordinary believers— clergy and laity alike—who have, on the one hand, new access to the resources of the Christian tradition not unlike those afforded by the printing press, but who, on the other, have access to technological means of connection, creativity, and collaboration with those resources that remained in the hands of a narrow elite even after the Protestant Reformations.

Unlike earlier church reforms, the Digital Reformation is driven not so much by theologies, dogmas, and politics—though these are certainly subject to renewed questioning—but by the digitally enhanced spiritual practices of ordinary believers with global access to each other and to all manner of religious knowledge previously available only to clergy, scholars, and other religious specialists. This pretty much puts everything in play—our traditions, our histories, our understanding of the sacred, even the structure and meaning of the sacred texts that we thought had been secured into an enduring canon way back in the fourth century.

The purpose of this book, then, is to provide insight into the opportunities and challenges presented by new digital social media for mainline churches, and to suggest ways that lay and ordained leaders in ministry—clergy, chaplains, community organizers, religious educators, social justice workers, spiritual caregivers, and so on—can participate in this Digital Reformation by way of nurturing and sustaining the Christian Church as a force for spiritual and social transformation.

By "mainline churches," I am referring for the most part to the so-called "Seven Sisters" of American Protestantism—American Baptists, Disciples of Christ, Congregationalists, Episcopalians,

Lutherans, Methodists, and Presbyterians.[1] But the book should also be of value to leaders in ministry from other denominations as well, particularly those who trace their denominational roots to the premodern or Reformation churches. I should note, too, that, in keeping with the distributed nature of digital social media itself, even within a mainline denominational framework, I understand "church" in relatively broad terms. Thus, I see the Church as extending from the institutionalized community that gathers in identifiable bricks-and-mortar structures to the less formally structured Body of Christ constituted by believers as they live out their faith in diverse ways in the world.

I approach this project from a decidedly historical and cultural perspective, setting the changes related to new digital media within the longer sweep of Church history. I take this approach because the Church, unlike other institutions that are also affected by recent technological changes, derives much of its identity from an explicit understanding of its development within the long sweep of human history. For people who see themselves as connected to a narrative of faith and hope that extends from the beginning of creation to the end of earthly time, attending to a phenomenon that seems to have sprung up over the last few years can feel like jumping onto the wave of a passing fad. Setting a new approach to communication, relationship, and community within the wider historical context of the Church allows us to see it in terms of continuities as well as differences. This, in turn, invites a deeper exploration of the Christian tradition for resources that will help us to more productively navigate and narrate what I believe is the most profound social and ecclesiological change encountered by the Church since the Protestant Reformation.

I also write from the perspective of a "digital optimist"— someone who believes that on balance the social benefits of digital technologies outweigh the very real risks. But I would nonetheless characterize myself as a "digital realist." So what I argue is that, like them or not, digital social media and mobile computing define the social reality with which we must contend if we are to participate in any meaningful way in the contemporary world. Thus, I see the challenge at the core of this book as developing a historically and culturally contextualized understanding of the impact of digital technologies on religion that balances an appropriate embrace of new ways of communicating, leading, and creating community with a deep appreciation for the resources of the Christian tradition that have long sustained believers through successive waves of cultural change.

What is the Digital Reformation?

A revitalization of the Church driven by the often ad hoc spiritualities of ordinary believers as they integrate practices of access, connection, participation, creativity, and collaboration, encouraged by the widespread use of new digital social media into all aspects of daily life, including the life of faith.

Indulgences of the Digital Reformation: What Digitally Integrated Religious Practice Looks Like

Of course, the signs and wonders of the Digital Reformation are everywhere. Indeed, many think of them as late modern indulgences that promise to smooth the path to whatever counts as redemption for believers and seekers today. And like the medieval indulgences that preceded the Bible as the first mass-produced product of Gutenberg's press, there are so many of them that it's almost impossible to keep up.

It seems that almost everywhere you turn on the internet, there are commentators considering the relative merits of online prayer, or of "tweeting" or "texting" during church services. All manner of advice is available on whether and how your church should have a presence on Facebook, Flickr, Twitter, and YouTube (a bit of it from me). Even the pope has directed Roman Catholic priests to dive into the digital domain.[2]

The increasing mobility of computing devices—lightweight laptops and tablet computers, smartphones, MP3 players (e.g., iPods), and portable gaming consoles—means that digital engagement is integrated into the fabric of daily life. No longer need we imagine the lonely geek sitting before the numbing glow of the computer screen, leaving behind the embodied uncertainties of "the real world" for the constructed delights of "virtual" reality. Virtual reality is embedded in physical reality to an ever-growing extent in the lives of most Westerners, Asians, and significant populations in the developing world. Internet access goes with most of us every-where we go, connecting us to friends and family with an ease that all but obliterates the anxieties of digital isolation that were at the root of Robert D. Putnam's 2000 bestseller, *Bowling Alone: The Collapse and Revival of American Community*. Indeed, research-ers from the University of Southern California and the University of Toronto have found an increase in friendships reported among American adults between the ages of twenty-five and seventy-four. This research indicated that heavy internet users have the most friends both on- and offline and, importantly, that these friendships are no more or less superficial than those tracked in previous studies.[3]

The blurring of the line between digital and physical reality has not passed religious life by, either. A church in Texas, for instance, hands out MP3 players to children attending worship services with their parents so that the kids can "hear the gospel in their own child language" while simultaneously "absorb[ing] the ritual and the hymns and the fellowship." The integration of digital resources and connectivity to others in daily life likewise impacts the spiri-tual lives of adults well beyond the bricks-and-mortar church. An Anglican priest in Nova Scotia has adapted a medieval practice of blessing farming equipment to offer "grace for gadgets": blessings for cell phones, laptops, and other digital tools of common work and life.[4]

Need some spiritual guidance to sort through the multiple, competing demands confronting you each day? There's an app for that. Dozens of them. A search on iTunes for iPhone applications with the keyword "Bible" yields hundreds of results; dozens more (some overlapping) come up for a search on "Jesus."[5] There are more mundane resources like the Bible (in various translations and a multitude of languages), the Episcopal *Book of Common Prayer*, and the Reformed *Westminster Confession of Faith*. But opportunities for easy access to spiritual encouragement, enrichment, and guidance go well beyond digitized traditional Christian meat-and-potatoes fare. The "Love Dare" app offers "fifty-two weekly [biblically based] dares to help you express love in your marriage." The Mormon "Bible Signs of the Times" app provides insight into more than sixty-five biblical signs predicting earthquakes, tsunamis, natural disasters, and wars along with information about the seven seals in Revelation. One of my favorites, the "Holy Roller" app, allows users with pressing spiritual questions to find scriptural wisdom that speaks to both "blessings" and "burdens" in their lives by scrolling through a list of topics such as inner peace, health, frustration, and courage. "Simply scroll through the Holy Roller to find what you are feeling," users are instructed, "hit next or shake your iPhone, and your scripture will appear." And that doesn't count the religiously themed music, movies, television shows, podcasts, audiobooks, and games with which the smartphone of today's tech-savvy believer might be stocked.[6]

Lest we mark digital religiosity as superficially social or theologically thin, we might also consider the treasure trove of academic theology that is now available, most of it at no cost, to seekers, believers, and critics around the globe through GoogleBooks, scholarly websites (for example, the American Academy of Religion or the Society for the Study of Biblical Literature), as well as digital religion magazines and blogs such as *Immanent Frame*, *Killing the Buddha*, and *Religion Dispatches*. Beyond this, up-to-the-minute religious commentary and reflection is available on a wide range of online versions of religious journals such as *Sojourners* and *Commonweal* as well as in religion sections of online secular news sites, including the *Washington Post* "On Faith" blog; the *Guardian* religion section; and the Australian Broadcasting Corporation's "Faith and Ethics" page. Add to this *Huffington Post* blogs by religion writers like Diana Butler Bass and James Martin, S.J., or academic theologian Serene Jones.

And let us not forget the numerous personal websites and blogs of leading scholars in religion, theology, and related fields (not to mention YouTube videos of their various public talks and classroom lectures) that provide insight into developing and published work, as well as career trajectories mapped in online *curriculum vitae*. Stanley Hauerwas's blog comes to mind, for instance, or Martin Marty's popular "Sightings." If you're not sure how to get to all this theological bounty, aggregation sites like *Religion News Service*, *Get Religion*, and *The Revealer* will help you sort through it all. A regular feed of headlines from the Faith in Public Life Center will keep you up-to-date on breaking religion news and emerging trends.

The sheer volume of opportunities to connect to others of similar religious affiliation or inclination and the range of material of religious interest now available in digital forms that can be accessed via the internet would seem to point to something of a resurgence in religious practice across almost all faith groups. From right-wing religious extremists, to New Age gurus, to fundamentalist New Atheists, and everything in between, digital media have clearly been at the center of a global explosion in religious creativity, conversation, critique, and cross-cultural connection over the past two decades. Even the Amish have an online newspaper.[7]

The New Revised Book of Numbers: Mainline Decline & Digital Possibility

Yet we also continuously hear the drumbeat of religious decline. Plummeting church membership and attendance since the 1950s is no longer news. Surveys by the Pew Forum on Religion & Public Life and Trinity College's "American Religious Identification Survey" (ARIS) have shown a continuing decline in religious identification over the past decade, with the steepest losses occurring in mainline Protestant denominations. The growth in religious "Nones"—people who answer "none" when asked with which religious tradition they identify—has been confirmed in 2010 Gallup polling.[8] All of this has of course been discouraging in traditional communities of faith struggling to maintain levels of membership and contribution that will sustain their ministries.

Hopeful examples of thriving mainline congregations notwithstanding, the data here is relatively unambiguous: as mainline Protestantism in all denominational forms has seen decades of declining membership in the United States and around the world, Evangelical,

non-denominational, Pentecostal, and other non-mainline Protestant denominations have retained a more stable level of membership in the United States and have steadily grown pretty much
everywhere else.[9] Indeed, the starkness of this reality has prompted
many social researchers to revise the demographic descriptor for
Congregational, Episcopal, Lutheran, Methodist, and Presbyterian
denominations from "mainline" to "oldline" Protestant.

In 1990, Americans who identified as Pentecostal or "generi-
cally Christian"—a designation that includes Evangelical and "born
again" Christians, and a range of non-denominational affiliations—
were roughly equal in number (18 percent) to those who identified
as mainline Protestants (18.7 percent).[10] Baptists, many of whom
share spiritual and political affinities with non-mainline Protestant
churches, made up a slightly larger proportion (19.3 percent) of
self-identified believers in 1990. By 2008, mainline Protestants had
dropped to 12.9 percent of the population, while Evangelicals, non-
denominational Christians, and Pentecostals held steady at 17.7 percent, with Baptists adding close to sixteen (15.8) percent to the total
(33.5 percent) population of non-mainline Protestants. Across the
same time period, the fastest growing group by religious identification was the so-called Nones. Researchers at the Pew Forum on Religion found that more than 20 percent of people with no self-defined
denominational identification have been drawn from the Anglican/
Episcopal and Congregationalist traditions.[11] [See Figure 1 below.]

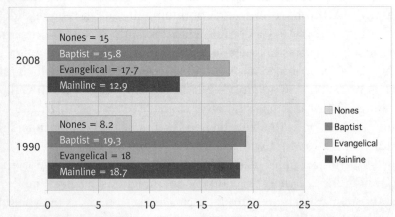

Figure 1: Self-Identification of U.S. Protestants and "Nones," 1990 vs. 2008

Still, the very same studies have also pointed to what may be a more subtle and profound reshaping of American faith practice that complicates questions of the viability and relevance of religion, perhaps especially of Christianity in its more moderate to progressive expressions. All of these recent surveys highlight the persistence of religious belief and spiritual practice in American culture. A scant 7 percent of those identifying as Nones in the ARIS population reported being atheists. Indeed, while Nones reported less certainty about religious questions, more than half expressed belief in some sort of higher power. Another 35 percent were classified as "hard" agnostics, who firmly reject the existence of a divinity or "soft" agnostics, who tend not to believe in the existence of a divinity, but who hold that the question cannot really be proved either way

Americans continue to engage in a wide variety of practices that they consider "spiritual" or "religious," and these practices are often informed by online engagements or are fully located in digital communities. A 2004 report by the Pew Internet & American Life Project showed a 94-percent increase over two years in the number of internet users seeking religious information online. While no survey data is currently available to update these earlier findings, it is reasonable to assume that the explosion of social media sites after 2006, when Facebook moved out of educational communities into corporate and personal networks, has only amplified digital religious exploration in an America in which more than 80 percent of homes have internet access. All of this suggests that the predominant religious issue in America seems to be related not so much to belief, but to belonging, and that in a particularly institutionalized sense associated with physical, built churches disconnected from the digitally integrated reality of contemporary life.[12]

Most of us in mainline traditions have gotten used to smelling that particularly bitter brand of coffee on Sunday mornings. I think we can all agree with Bishop Kirk Smith, quoted in the preface of this book, that we have pretty much "blown it" with regard to engaging the dominant modes of communication of the modern age to share our vision of Christian life with Americans and others around the world. The good news, however, is that the very characteristics that have made mainline Protestants so generally ineffective with broadcast media are actually assets with regard to digital social media, which highlight practices of creative improvisation, participation, and distributed authority. New digital communication practices provide the opportunity to share the riches of ancient and medieval Christian traditions that ground much of mainline religious practice while also opening our churches to the diverse spiritual perspectives of the many believers and seekers who, while they may not wear Episcopalian, Lutheran, Methodist, or Presbyterian badges on their sleeves, are nonetheless engaged by religious questions as they respond to the challenges of life in the wired world today.

So it is that we find ourselves in the midst of a dramatic cultural and social change, one that has impacted nearly every aspect of our lives—our work, our relationships with family and friends, and certainly our religious practice both in worship settings and in the context of day-to-day spirituality. Through the summer of 2010, a chorus of scholars and pundits shared new cognitive, physiological, and behavioral evidence that insists we sharpen our focus on the enduring effects of digital engagement on our identities, our relationships, and the physiology of our brains themselves.[13] These critiques are matched by equally compelling evidence showing the ways in which new digital social media and mobile computing platforms are contributing to the cause of global social, political, and economic liberation to an extent that would have been unimaginable less than a decade ago.[14] The back and forth of it all is head-spinning.

In fact, the pace and scope of social change related to global access to new digital social media has seemed so overwhelming that Reboot, a group of Jewish professionals, sponsored a "National Day of Unplugging" in the spring of 2010 during which people were encouraged to turn off all electronic media devices and tune in to unwired connections to their families, communities, nature, faith, and the unmediated whispers of their own hearts.[15] It is clear that life in these heady, early days of the Digital Reformation is marked by an intemperance in our use of digital media, both social and informational, that we surely must check. Efforts to "unplug" are laudable when they invite us to reflect on the transformation in which we are currently participating so that we can make better choices about how we live our lives in the context of our most important relationships and most deeply held beliefs. But they are misguided when they contribute to the illusion that the effects of digital culture on our daily lives, including our religious or spiritual practice, are something from which we can truly opt out, even temporarily.

To put it another way, whether you do or do not own or drive a car, you participate in the ascendency of automobiles in American life and culture that occurred at the turn of the last century—a change that remapped the American landscape and psyche as surely as the meteoric growth of digital media on mobile devices is changing American culture today.

Clicking Ahead: How This Book Is Organized

In *Tweet If You ♥ Jesus* I attempt to develop a picture of what is an impossibly complex reality by first offering a social, cultural, and historical perspective on digital social media (in Part I) before turning to three areas of particular concern in the Church: communication (in Part II), community (in Part III), and leadership (in Part IV). I draw these reflections together in two short case studies (in Part V) that illustrate how differences in church history and theology shape communication styles, leadership practices, and life in community in ways that make the digital landscape more congenial to mainline churches than broadcast platforms could ever have been.

The chapters that follow will also reveal what is the central dilemma in the structuring of this book. That is, while I have attempted to organize the book around the themes of communication, community, and leadership as though these were separable constructs, it quickly becomes clear that they are not. Practices of communication are the foundation for all of our relationships with others, so any conversation about communication is bound to overlap with discussions of the relationships that make up communities and the ways of relating that constitute leadership.

This overlap is in fact highlighted by the linguistic relationship among the words "communication," "community," and, for that matter, "communion," all coming into the English language by way of the Latin verb *communicare*—"to share, divide out, impart, inform, join, unite, participate in." The Latin root of communication is itself an adaptation of an earlier term, *communis*, "to make common, to share among all or many."[16] When we talk about communication, then, we are really talking about the deepest social and spiritual roots of community and the practices necessary for creating, sustaining, and extending community. The structure described below is an attempt to mark out dynamic, mutually reinforcing phenomena so that we can examine them more closely, and you will surely see much slippage between one concept and the next in the course of the discussion that follows.

Part I: Introducing Habitus

Part I introduces the concept of *habitus**—a term used by sociologists to describe the matrix of beliefs, attitudes, dispositions, preferences, behaviors, postures, gestures, material resources, and so on that characterize the culture of a particular time and place.[17] Literally, from its Latin root, *habere*, a habitus is the complex sense of how we hold ourselves in relation to others in the world. And, not for nothing, it is a term that connects early and medieval Christian understandings of the relationship between inward dispositions and outward expressions of faith to contemporary explorations of what it means to be human in community.

When a medieval nun or monk "took the habit," she or he was not committing merely to wear unflattering clothing and sensible shoes for life. The monastic habitus required a comprehensive commitment to a way of life oriented toward activities that nurtured and expressed Christian beliefs and that reinforced the hierarchical structure of the Church. When we examine a habitus, we're not just looking at an idea or even a paradigm; we're not just looking at change across historical time. Examining a habitus allows us to understand ourselves, our communities, and our culture within a holistic rather than linear narrative.

In Chapter 1, we explore the concept of habitus so that we can approach the impact of technological change on daily life, including

---

* The singular and plural of "habitus" are spelled the same (like "deer").

the life of faith, with greater practical complexity. We extend this exploration in Chapter 2 by sampling Western Christian habitus from the Middle Ages to the present day in order to develop greater fluency in a contemporary digital habitus. This discussion will serve as the backdrop for deeper exploration of communication, community, and leadership in the Digital Reformation in the remainder of the book.

What is Habitus?

The matrix of beliefs, attitudes, dispositions, preferences, behaviors, postures, gestures, material resources, and so on that characterize the culture of a particular time and place. The common understanding of "how things work around here."

Part II: Communication & the Digital Reformation

Concerns that mainline Christians have missed opportunities to connect with wider communities of believers and seekers through radio and television tend to situate new digital technologies along a continuum of broadcast and other mass media communications forms. This seems obvious enough: The radio gave audio voice to the words written on the pages of books and newspapers. The motion picture added moving images to the stories we could tell, and this capability was extended into the day-to-day domestic lives of most North Americans and Westerners through, as Lawrence Welk would say, "the magic of television." The logical extension of this trajectory has been to see the development of the internet and associated social media in one-to-many broadcast terms, as another evolutionary step in the ability of institutionally authorized individuals to send messages out to ever more consumers. In this assessment, what the internet added to the broadcast communication portfolio was the ability to connect not only with more people, but to do so quickly and globally at dramatically reduced production costs.

In fact, especially in the context of evolving social media and mobile computing, the internet is not merely *a thing* we use to get a message out to more people, but rather *a place* we enter to engage others.

That's good news for mainline churches, which tend to carry in our DNA important markers for transparency in communications, collaboration in leadership, and distributed ministry—tools that position us for much greater success with new digital social media than we have had with broadcast media. This doesn't take broadcast and other top-down, mass-market communication out of the picture, but it significantly turns down the volume.

In Chapter 3, then, we look at premodern social media practices associated with reading *before* the invention of the printing press in order to identify resources from within our tradition to apply to communication in the Digital Reformation. Chapter 4 highlights the differences between broadcast and digital communication practices. The chapter goes on to consider how the apostle Paul used communication practices to nurture spiritual health in the communities of the early Church that are particularly applicable to life in the communities of the Digital Reformation.

Part III: Community in the Digital Reformation

It may once have been true, as the old joke goes, that Protestantism is the only faith tradition that multiplies by dividing. Using a famously (or infamously) broad definition of "denomination," the editors of the *World Christian Encyclopedia* claimed in 2001 that in the centuries since the Lutheran Reformation, some nine thousand Protestant denominations have emerged across the world, along with another twenty-two thousand "independent" denominations.[18] For many, the Digital Age promises to exacerbate this disintegration, enabling each of us to access the spiritual resources she finds most attractive by way of crafting an idiosyncratic spirituality that may provide much personal comfort but little of the encouragement necessary to advocate on behalf of and care for others. As more and more people leave our churches, we often see contemporary fascination with digitally tricked-out smartphones and sleek new go-anywhere laptops and tablet computers as tools for the erosion of Christian community that began when Christian radio and television allowed people to praise the Lord in their jammies.

Yet we are hardly the first generation of Christians to struggle with how to sustain spiritually vibrant communities formed by diverse individuals from multicultural backgrounds. In Chapter 5, then, we will see how broadcast communication practices have often tended to create the illusion of community while undermining its practice in the Church and the everyday world.

New digital social media do more, however, than enhance existing communities. They also play an important role in extending spiritual relatedness beyond the local church. The critical element of reform here is that digital media invite a kind of 24/7 engagement that was very much part of the life of the Church prior to the modern era. Chapter 6, thus, takes up digital practices of witness, bridging, and engagement with others that enrich existing communities while also extending the Church's radical welcome to the marginalized within the Church and to believers and seekers who live outside of defined spiritual community.

Part IV: Leadership for the Digital Reformation

In the chapters ahead, we'll see that leadership in the Digital Reformation is significantly different than it was in the past. This change hinges on the transformation of authority that is itself driven by the widely distributed, bottom-up access to knowledge and the means for producing and distributing knowledge associated with new digital social media. Being known as a leader in the Digital Reformation, then, does not so much depend on whether or not you wear a collar, what color your shirt might be, or what your title is, as much as it does on your ability to effectively participate in or establish wider conversational spaces where others are encouraged to share their own perspectives.

In the Digital Reformation, communication practices allow a new manifestation of leadership to emerge within the context of collaborative, overlapping, distributed communities. *Any* of the individuals who participate in a conversation might emerge as a "thought leader." Likewise, anyone's humble Facebook page could become a hub for conversation, serving as a temporary leadership forum in that digital space. Or, consider the case in Iran in the summer of 2009, when protestors posted news and video on Facebook and Twitter throughout election fraud protests. A group of more or less nameless social media "reporters" became the leading voice on that issue, shaping perception across the World Wide Web, including in the popular, broadcast media.

These new practices challenge longstanding concepts of leadership drawn largely from modern, industrial management models. In Chapter 7, we will consider the ways in which the Reformation histories of mainline Protestants prepare us for more distributed, relational practices of leadership for the Digital Reformation. Chapter 8, in turn, shares examples of contemporary and ancient leaders in ministry who have created very different locales for leadership in the wide and thriving borders between institutional authority and individual charisma.

Part V: Practicing Reformation

Clearly, there is much we can do to improve our effectiveness with new media as both tools and locales for renewing Christian community. In Chapter 9, I draw together the work we've done in the previous sections to examine the digital presence of two very different churches and three very different leaders in ministry.

These are early days in the Digital Reformation, so no one has it exactly right. But the case studies offered in Part V illustrate how practices of listening, attending, connecting, and engaging that draw from our deepest traditions can move effectively from face-to-face to digital settings. These interlaced practices are summarized in the model described below, which aims to link durable Christian traditions to the more improvisational practices that characterize much of life in the Digital Reformation.

Lacing Up for the Reformation

Throughout this book, I will make the case that the technologies at play in the Digital Reformation invite us back to ways of relating, sharing, and creating meaning together that were all but lost as the sweep of modern progress moved into the Broadcast Age. While these social technologies can often seem impossibly complicated, the core practices they encourage are not far off from those that animated medieval faith communities. For convenience, I think of these practices—listening, attending, connecting, engaging—as forming a kind of "lace" that symbolizes the interaction among the fundamental spiritual practices of the Digital Reformation.

Now, I am of course thinking here of a medieval lace, which would have been a simple knotted braid that nonetheless formed intricate patterns with great symbolic meaning. More ornate laces of the sort that adorn the dresses of women in Renaissance masterpieces are most often the products of early modern machinery that spun its way into the mass production practices of the Industrial Age. But handmade lace of the kind that was treasured in the Middle Ages reflected, as John Ruskin opined in the nineteenth century, "a beauty which has been the reward of industry and attention."[19]

Woven through broader categories of communication, community, and leadership practice are more subtle practices of listening, attending, connecting, and engaging that might be imagined as something like a Celtic Trinity knot:

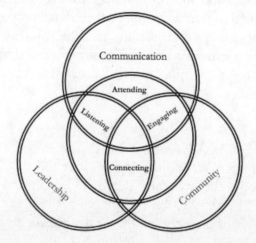

The dynamic, relational interplay symbolized by the Trinity lace is part of our deepest theology and spirituality as Christians—our habitus. Its core elements will be illustrated throughout the remaining chapters of *Tweet If You ♥ Jesus*. I will briefly summarize them here as they apply to digital practices for ministry before we move on to see them at work both in our history and in contemporary practices by leaders in ministry who are taking up the challenges and opportunities presented by digital social media today.

Listening

The Greek philosopher Epictetus gave us the adage, "We have two ears and one mouth so that we can listen twice as much as we speak." This wisdom applies as much in digital space as in physical space. As we'll see, you're not a creepy stalker if you take some time to visit the Facebook pages, Twitter feeds, blogs, and websites of the people in your digital networks. You're getting to know people and you're getting to know the lay of the digital landscape you inhabit with them.

People put up pictures and list their interests because they want other people to see how they see themselves and the worlds they inhabit. So it's okay to look at the groups people "like" on Facebook or the lists they follow on Twitter. It's fine to click on the "information" tab and see what someone has decided to share about their education or their job. It's totally cool to watch the video they posted of their vacation or their daughter's graduation—not by way of gathering marketing data, but by way of trying to understand what matters to them. If you've ever said to someone at coffee hour, "Tell me a little bit about yourself," you know exactly how to do this.

Attending

Listening is part of attending, but it's not the whole of it. "To attend," beyond the standard dictionary definition of "paying attention to," means "to be present with," "to notice," "to be ready for service or ministry to." In the digital world, attending can be as simple as clicking "like" on someone's Facebook page. Two of my favorite Facebook friends, Hans-Christian Kasper and Margaret Benefiel, have elevated the Facebook "like" to a kind of digital spiritual practice, making the rounds among their friends and "waving" to them through the day. Kiwi liturgist Bosco Peters—who has some eighty thousand followers on Twitter—manages to be particularly gracious about greeting people who follow him, thanking people who retweet his tweets, and, on both Twitter and Facebook, acknowledging people whose tweets and posts find their way into his feed.

A lot of "attending," then, comes down to just being polite and kind in digital space in the same do-as-you-would-have-others-do ways you would want to practice in a face-to-face setting. The digital version of Paul's repeated instruction that we "greet each other with a holy kiss" (Romans 16:16, 1 Corinthians 16:20, 2 Corinthians 13:12, 1 Thessalonians 5:26) seems to play out in these small gestures, as well as in what I've come to think of as micro-ethical digital practices of honesty and acknowledgement when reposting or retweeting material you found on someone else's page. Especially for leaders in ministry, this digital attentiveness powerfully models Christian love of neighbor in an environment where many people rightly worry (though often over much) about declining moral standards.

Connecting

In the world of social networking, "connecting" is usually where people want to start. On Facebook, connecting is more or less a requirement if you're going to be able to listen or attend to anyone. On Twitter, you can "follow" anyone you want, and many of the kindest among them will follow you back. The trick in either case is not to set yourself up like Socrates, tweeting and posting your wisdom and waiting for disciples to gather around you. Jesus invited children to gather around him (Matthew 19:13–15), but he pretty much hoofed it out to everyone else. Even the Sermon on the Mount (Matthew 5:1–7:29) was part of an extended road trip that allowed Jesus to encounter people he didn't already know.

The majority of people in my social media networks are friends, family members, colleagues, and less intimate associates whom I hope to know better over time. But there are also people who disagree with my point of view on things, who irritate me from time to time, and whom I just don't like. Which makes these networks as a whole not unlike the Church. As it turns out, in the social media world (as in the rest of life), whoever amasses the largest number of friends and followers does not "win." Still, it is a huge part of the vocations of people who understand themselves as leaders in ministry to ensure that everyone who asks has a place at the table, digital or otherwise. Social media platforms don't invite the development of exclusive cocktail parties. They're more like pick-up games in a giant, global park. Everybody gets to play, though there's nothing wrong with helping people to figure out what spot is best suited to their interests and gifts. Connecting as generously as we are reasonably able expresses an important spiritual value to fellow travelers in the Digital Reformation.

Engaging

Appropriate practices of listening, attending, and connecting ground meaningful engagement in social media contexts in the same ways they do in face-to-face settings. Once you understand the interests of people in your core network, sharing content that is meaningful to them enriches relationship. One of the valuable lessons we learned from the medieval mystic Julian of Norwich, who could see the whole of God's creation in something as small as a hazelnut, applies here: Less is very often more. Sometimes—especially when you're discerning how many tweets and Facebook posts to log in a day—it's everything.

All of this is part of a practice of participating in social media spaces by way of building relationships that deepen and extend community rather than messaging or marketing your church, organization, or cause. People want to be known, and they want to know you. Personally, not institutionally.

Tweet If You ♥ Jesus approaches new media and the Church by situating contemporary religious practice within a historical, cultural, and social narrative and then exploring the implications of this narrative for the life of the Church in the Digital Reformation. A key assumption here is that for mainline churches to participate meaningfully in the revitalization of the Church, we must travel through this new landscape on its own terms, open throughout to the possibility that God just might be doing an entirely new thing among us—140 characters at a time.

Of course, by the time you are reading this book, it is likely that much of the technology I will discuss in the following chapters will have changed dramatically, or will have been rendered obsolete by some newly enchanting online forum or mobile gadget. As I write, Google is making aggressive moves to unseat Facebook as the dominant social media portal. The gossip in my Silicon Valley dog park is that Apple is developing a more affordable version of the iPhone that will allow it to enter wider markets in the United States and abroad through multiple cellular carriers. In the course of researching and writing this book, the Facebook profile page has been changed no fewer than five times. In 2001, one of the earliest writers on digital technologies and religion prophesied, "Electronic pets are, at most, a decade away."[20] It could happen. Maybe as you're reading this, your new iPooch 6G is snoozing at your feet. Who can say what's next?

ANGELO LOPEZ 2010

Fortunately, this is not a book on how to use new digital social media from a technical perspective (though the resource list on my website, www.elizabethdrescher.net, does provide links to helpful technical guidance on major digital social media platforms). Rather, in *Tweet If You ♥ Jesus*, we will explore the broader cultural challenge presented to leaders in ministry interested in engaging the potential of new digital social media for positive transformation in the Church.

Tweet If You ♥ Jesus is ultimately a book about paradox and possibility—about new ways of connecting, collaborating, and creating that will likely dismantle many of the familiar structures of the Church even as they carry with them the promise that believers and seekers today will be most able to be faithful stewards of the rich traditions of Christianity by serving as facilitators of spiritually meaningful transformation. Can we really do other than be honored and awed that God is acting through us now, in all our confusion and curiosity about the rapidly developing Digital Age, to shape the Church for future generations?

Part I

UNDERSTANDING HABITUS

KICKING THE HABIT

The Complicated Technology of Cultural Change

> We might possess every technological resource . . . but if our language is inadequate, our vision remains formless, our thinking and feeling are still running in the old cycles, our process may be "revolutionary" but not transformative.
>
> —*Adrienne Rich*

A YouTube video called "Medieval Helpdesk (with English subtitles)"[1] has entertained more than 2.6 million viewers since it made the leap from the Norwegian sitcom "Øystein og jeg" (Oystein and I) to the digital domain in 2007. In it, a sullen medieval monk, Brother Ansgar, sits alone in a candlelit hovel, a dark block on the desk before him. Shortly, there is a knock on the door, whereupon a smartly dressed young man enters and begins to help the monk to engage the mystery block. We see immediately that the object that vexes Brother Ansgar is a book, the "new system" that has the helpdesk technician running all over the monastery troubleshooting. Brother Ansgar, who is skilled with the traditional scroll, struggles with opening the book, turning pages, and finding his place again after the book has been closed. Although the book comes with a compact users' manual, this, too, is in book format, and poor Brother Ansgar cannot use it, either.

The video, which has been translated into a much less entertaining English version, copied in various YouTube reenactments,
and, more recently, adapted into a one-act play, is funny precisely
because it so faithfully captures our frustrations with new technologies and the condescending technical support that often comes with
them. The video brilliantly illustrates the personal, social, intellectual, and emotional effects of what might appear to be a very
small technical or material change. The wise and knowing monk is
reduced to receiving infantilizing instruction from a young techno-
scribe. More than Knut Nærum, the writer of the original skit,
might have been aware, this reversal of roles—the young teaching
the old—would have represented a profound cultural change in the
Middle Ages, new technology notwithstanding.

This particular shift did not of course occur in the Middle Ages,
but it is happening regularly now, in the early days of the Digital
Reformation. How many of us rely on teenagers or young adults for
both technical skill coaching and general insight on the workings
of computers, smartphones, the internet, and social media sites?
While the dominance of youth has been growing in the U.S. popular culture at least since the end of World War II, it is only since
the recent ascendency of digital technology that youthful inventors
and day-to-day technology educators have come to be seen more as
ordinary kids than as prodigies.

As in the case of hapless Brother Ansgar, a focus on the expertise of young people is but one indicator of a shift that is not only
technological, but also cultural. Certainly the cultural changes we
will explore in this book are related to technological changes, but
their impact reaches far beyond the words and images on Facebook,
Twitter, and other social media pages that weave new narratives of
personal, social, and, for many of us, spiritual identity. Our ability
to turn the page, as it were, on a new era of religious practice in
which mainline churches have continuing relevance will depend on
our ability to understand the changes associated with new digital
media in specifically social and cultural terms. In this first chapter, then, we look in more detail at a socio-cultural framework
for understanding technological change—the concept of habitus
as a matrix of commonly held attitudes, ideas, ways of thinking,

actions, gestures, and dispositions as well as material markers of "the way things are" in a particular time and place. Understanding the ways in which new digital social media are shaping what is clearly a radical shift in the dominant habitus of North American culture, and across Western culture more generally, opens the possibility for mainline churches to participate in this change in ways that nurture positive transformation.

Opening the Manual: The Structure of Habitus

Pierre Bourdieu, probably the most influential contemporary thinker on the concept, described habitus as "the principle generating and unifying all practices."[2] Our everyday actions in relation to one another have the effect of reinforcing what we all generally assume to be true, adapting it, or challenging it through both intentional and accidental actions. Everyone participates, like it or not. One way to think of a habitus is as something like an internalized manual of "standard operating procedures" combined with an externalized collection of "tools of the trade" for ordinary life.

Still, we don't usually have access to a manual or some other guide that provides a wider perspective on the habitus in which we are immersed. We can never be quite sure exactly how the habitus is structured or whether, how, or when our ideas, activities, and interactions will, on their own or in aggregation with those of others, have an impact on the generally accepted understanding of "normal life." This can make change seem somewhat random or chaotic, and that, in turn, can amplify our anxiety about what change might bring while dampening our enthusiasm for the possibilities it opens.

We do, however, have artifacts from the past that function as something like manuals for the habitus in operation in other times and places. Among the most accessible habitus guides are the monastic "rules of life" developed in late antiquity and the early Middle Ages by, for example, St. Augustine, St. Pachomious, St. Bridget, and, most famously, St. Benedict. These rules for common life stand out as articulations of an idealized, if not always realized, habitus precisely because they were set out in distinction from the more common

culturally accepted practices of their day, which novices renounced
as they entered into life in community. And, of course, most of us
today are separated from monastic rules both by our non-monastic
vocations and further still by the passage of time, so the practices
described in monastic rules are all the more distinct to us.

The Benedictine Rule remains the most influential monastic
rule.[3] Written in the early Middle Ages, it is exquisitely detailed
in its attention to the spiritual and liturgical aspects of monastic
life that might seem to be the point of joining a religious order. Far
beyond this, however, the Rule handles with great care the practices of communication, community, and leadership that develop
out of day-to-day interactions over meals, in the course of shared
work, and in the making of decisions and resolution of disputes.
Benedict goes so far as to advise his charges on sleep cycles and
bathroom breaks that will allow for greater attentiveness in prayer
by ensuring proper digestion. This extensive spiritual and material
thoughtfulness is required because the life that Benedictine monks
take up insists on a studied vigilance against the ordinary, non-
monastic habitus left behind. Only a detailed understanding of and
rigid obedience to the Rule, from which even an abbot or abbess
is not exempt, will allow monks and nuns in training to kick the
habitus of secular life.

Benedictine monk or not, poor Brother Ansgar would surely
have had extensive training in his youth and later professional
practice involving the use of the scroll as an authoritative container
of knowledge. These years of practice would have contributed not
only to how he tended to think about things, but also how he physically interacted with such a container for information—his "muscle
memory," as athletes would say today. And his engagement with
the scroll would have participated in the structuring of his relationships with other readers and non-readers.

If we studied monastic rules as they were written and rewritten
over the centuries, up to the present day, we would learn much
about how the habitus of religious communities has changed over
time. Even in revisions striving to be faithful to the original visions
of the founders of monastic orders, we would see adaptations, for
example, to the development of Protestantism, to changes in the

status of women, and, most recently, to more active participation of laypeople in monastic communities. In the process, we would certainly learn much about changes in the larger culture, too, but through a necessarily narrow, intentionally counter-culture lens.

Reformation Ready-to-Wear: How Habitus is Signaled

The thing about an ordinary, non-monastic habitus—the beauty of it, really—is that we rarely afford it as much thought as did Benedict and his followers. The commonly held assumptions, attitudes, dispositions, behaviors, and material objects that make it clear to an outsider that we belong to this place and time seem to make sense to us on their own. Clothing, for instance, plays a big part in the structuring of a habitus. This is precisely how the garb worn by vowed religious came to be called "habits" in the first place. But those of us with less restrictive dress codes are no less constrained by cultural norms with regard to what we wear. We may have more options than did Sally Field's *Flying Nun* character, Sister Bertrille, but they are nonetheless organized around clearly defined categories for relatively specific purposes. Among many other things, clothes mark our gender, our age, our class, our tolerance for difference, something of our usual geographical locale, our nationality, and, as we recall from Jesus' parable of the wedding banquet (Matthew 22), our regard for the occasion to which we have been called.

Still, however much we might fuss over exactly the right thing to wear to work, school, church, or to this or that event, we don't usually have to think each day about the range of attire that would be considered appropriate in those settings. Nor, for that matter, do we consider whether or not clothing is needed at all. We don't, that is, get up in the morning wondering if or how we should cover our nakedness so we can get on with the day lest we be cast out into the darkness with weeping and gnashing of teeth. (Okay, maybe Lady Gaga does, but let's call her The Exception That Proves the Rule.)

Like clothing, other material resources demonstrate our participation in the prevailing habitus of a time and place. The kinds of homes we live in, the types of furniture that we buy, the foods we eat, the music listened to by various subsets of our cultural community, and so on all let others know that we're from here rather than there, that we live in the present rather than the past or the future.

Cup Holders for the Reformation:
The Slow Ride to Changes in Habitus

That said, it is important to note that *a habitus isn't subconscious*, and it's not just a set of intellectual ideas and assumptions—a paradigm (though a habitus does include the currently reigning paradigms). "How things are in these parts" is not some deep, dark secret folded into the origami of the neocortex. Rather, a habitus is the whole structure of resources and practices—ideas and assumptions, certainly, but also activities, symbols, class boundaries, stories, rituals, and so on—that are available to us as we navigate our way through life. As with a routine route to work, we could describe it in great detail if asked, but after a zillion or so back and forths, we don't need to be all that attentive to our attentiveness. It *seems* like we're "on autopilot," but we're really not. We simply have no need to be particularly reflective about the matrix of practices that make up ordinary, day-to-day living. Psychologists refer to this kind of "on tap" knowledge as "preconscious" or "pre-reflective" knowledge. It is the basic stuff of a habitus.

Another thing about a habitus that makes it different from, say, a passing social trend is that it is simultaneously durable and malleable. That is, a habitus extends over time, shaping our life experiences even as we, individually and collectively, subtly reshape the dominant cultural habitus through our imperfect, innovative, and sometimes impertinent practice of it.

Do you remember when, for instance, on your pre-reflective drive to and from work, cup holders became standard equipment in automobiles? If you were driving in the 1950s and '60s, they weren't there at all, other, perhaps, than as a slight indentation on the inside of the door of your glove compartment. You might flip the glove box open when you stopped to eat at a drive-in restaurant, but you'd certainly never drive around with a full cup of piping hot coffee. Anyone with the slightest common sense knew that was dangerous!

Nevertheless, the idea of sipping from a cup of joe on the way to work started sounding not so bad, and a series of more or less clunky options for drinking while driving developed over the next decade or so to quench this particular thirst. If, like me, you learned to drive in the late 1970s, you perhaps had one of those oh-so-attractive plastic lasso cup holders that you hooked on the inside of the front door. And, if your dad was anything like mine, you were routinely lectured about how dangerous that innocent device was any time you forgot to take it out of the family station wagon along with your 8-track tapes.

It would take until the late 1980s for cup holders to become standard equipment on cars for both drivers and passengers. The change was propelled not by new engineering insights, but by how people were actually using cars. Their innovative practice—what they did with the available resources—changed not only the automobile itself and the experience of driving, but also the process of designing cars and a life practice as basic as eating. Consuming entire meals in the car has by now become routine, helped along by greater accommodation to solitary, mobile dining built into the late modern car used in the context of longer drives from suburban homes to urban jobs. These commonplace practices of dining while driving speak volumes about our relationship to food, to our work, and to one another and mark a dramatic shift in the general American habitus over the course of the last half-century.

The cup holder didn't cause this shift on its own, but it certainly participated in it in a big way. So goes the complicated technology of cultural change at a slow, almost imperceptible pace over time, with remarkably little fanfare despite an extensive impact on diverse aspects of our lives. The "nothing much" that is the innovation of the built-in cup holder points, on the one hand, to a complex network of changes that have occurred throughout our everyday lives. On the other, a Prius is still recognizable as a car even to someone who came of age behind the wheel of a '63 Ford Falcon. That is, the complicated practice of automobile transportation, along with the practice of eating, has proved both durable and malleable. Thus, even as a habitus is changed by the intentional and accidental practices of ordinary people in the course of their everyday lives, other aspects of it are reinforced in the course of those same practices.

SOME CHARACTERISTICS OF HABITUS	
HABITUS *IS*	HABITUS IS *NOT*
A matrix of commonly held attitudes, beliefs, ways of thinking, ideas, paradigms, behaviors, gestures, actions, dispositions, material objects	A paradigm or idea
Pre-conscious knowledge	Subconscious knowledge
Holistic	Linear
Both durable and malleable	Fixed and eternal
Both reinforced and reshaped by intentional and accidental actions	Changed in total by sudden insight or fiat

How Many Mainline Protestants Does It Take to Screw in a Reformation?: Defining Habitus in Your Community

There's a constantly evolving series of light bulb jokes that circulates among churchy types that never seems to fail to garner a chuckle when the denominationally appropriate one is tossed into a sermon. *How many Presbyterians does it take to screw in a light bulb? None. God has predestined when the lights will be on. Episcopalians? Don't touch that light bulb! My great-grandmother donated that light bulb!* Corny though these old jokes might be, they are nonetheless valuable markers of the habitus of a particular community. Before we consider the evolution of cultural habitus in the next chapter, it might be worthwhile to note the markers of habitus in your community.

What are the key stories that shape how you understand yourself as a community? What are the stories you share with visitors or newcomers to give them a sense of "how things are" in your community? How have these stories changed over time? What artifacts represent what you might think of as the essential character of your community? What practices in your common life have gone out of style or come into favor over time? Are there small changes that have turned out to make a big difference in how you function as a community? What does the way change is handled or conflicts are addressed say about who you are as a community of faith? What seems most durable? What is more malleable?

Exploring such questions as they are illustrated in our larger history is a key first step in understanding the simultaneously emerging, blended, and conflicting habitus of a faith community and the practices of communication and leadership that can support and sustain that community as it grows into the future. In the next chapter we begin facing this future by looking more closely into our shared past.

2

HABITUS BY THE BOOK

From Medieval Obedience to Digital Improvisation

The future enters into us, in order to transform itself in us, long before it happens.

—Rainer Maria Rilke

A habitus, as we've seen, is a remarkably intricate thing. It is matrixed across different dimensions of ordinary life. It lasts in recognizable ways over time, but is also reshaped through everyday practice, including both intentional and accidental actions. As it is lived out in any particular moment, there cannot be any one authoritative description of it, and our own understanding of how the habitus of our culture works is largely preconscious. All of this makes it difficult to hone in on a description of a habitus that is neither overwhelmingly complex nor narrowly reductionistic.

In the previous chapter, I noted that monastic rules provide some of the best documented descriptions of habitus available to us. However, as I also noted, monastic rules reflect the engagement of monks and nuns with the world outside their communities, but they are specifically designed in contrast to practices of faith and life of the ordinary believers of interest to us here. Indeed, commentators today who encourage us to return to the more reflective, contemplative practices of the Middle Ages make the mistake of applying the habitus of the monastic few to the everyday lives of the majority ordinary believers, whose lives were marked with a complexity and distraction that accompanied living in relatively small, thin-walled, open spaces with extended family and often farm animals. Just try cultivating the life of the mind or stillness of soul with granny snoring next to you, a couple milk cows, some chickens, and pigs downstairs, and the neighbors in the throes of a loud, drunken row. Which is to say that monastic rules can teach us much about how a habitus works, but they are hardly guides to life in general. Getting to the religious or spiritual habitus of ordinary life in the Digital Reformation requires that we take a somewhat different approach.

Fortunately, there are two areas where we tend to make the core elements of "normal" practices of life in a particular time and place very clear: primary education and rituals of initiation, particularly religious ones. Primary education provides a child's entrée into civil culture just as religious ceremonies like baptism and confirmation are invitations into a community of believers for infants and early teens. At least since the Enlightenment—the intellectual engine of the modern era—both have usually been very well documented, including rationales for changing practices. So, documents and other artifacts from historical and contemporary educational and religious practice tend to provide a reliable and reasonably substantive picture of the general habitus of a given culture.

Although it may be quite interesting to look at religious initiation rites, getting to what might pass for an "essential" description of baptism among mainline churches pretty much defined by their differences on such matters would be no mean feat. Also, because most Christian initiation rites have at their roots very ancient practices filtered through successive interpretations, it takes a fair amount of work to sort through the layers of cultural meaning at play. And, that work would make for an entirely different book. For our purposes, an overview of educational practices from the Middle Ages to the present day will offer sufficient insight into shifts in the dominant cultural habitus that impact how we engage new digital social media in the context of religious practice. What we will see over time is a movement from an ancient and medieval—or premodern—habitus of *regulated obedience* to one characterized in the modern period by *regulated discovery and invention*, and finally, to a digital habitus of *regulated improvisation* at work in the late modern era in which we currently find ourselves.

Very briefly, these modes of habitus are distinguished by the relationship between the set of cultural regulations—"the rule"—and the intended effect of actions in relation to that rule. Likewise, in each habitus, change is introduced in somewhat different ways. While accidents, errors, and mistakes will always introduce the possibility of change into a habitus, through much of human history, change has been seen as a bad or dangerous thing to be avoided as much as possible. Even through the innovations of the Enlightenment, change was seen as something to be closely managed in order to avoid risk and maximize gain. It is only very recently that change has been seen as desirable in itself and that "resistance to change" has been considered something that had to be dealt with in order to move on to better things. These characteristics of habitus, which are summarized in the table below, play out in the stories of each age and every community.

TIME PERIOD	DOMINANT HABITUS	EFFECT OF PRACTICE	MODE OF CHANGE
Premodern	Regulated Obedience	Reinforce the Rule	Accidental/ Not Desired
Modern	Regulated Discovery and Invention	Extend the Rule	Strategic/Managed
Late Modern	Regulated Improvisation	Revise the Rule	Unpredictable/ Desired

A Saint for Slackers: The Habitus of Obedience

The seventh-century English saint Erkenwald, the bishop of London from 675 to 693, is hardly known today. However, back in the day, he was regarded as quite the miracle-worker. Mostly, these were healing miracles. Erkenwald, himself apparently a chronic gout sufferer—hence his status as the patron saint of those afflicted with gout—undertook visitations in his diocese on a horse cart.

According to the Venerable Bede, Erkenwald's cart, which was preserved by his followers, cured "people afflicted with fevers and other complaints" through proximity to the cart itself or to splinters cut from the cart that were carried home to the ailing.[1]

Not bad. However, the seldom-read collection of Erkenwald's miracles also includes the story of a quite different sort of miracle involving a slacker student and his utterly pedagogically appropriate—if you lived in medieval Christendom—schoolmaster, Elwin. According to Arcoid of London, a canon of St. Paul's Cathedral who collected the *Miracles of St. Erkenwald* in the first half of the twelfth century,[2] Master Elwin was a dedicated teacher, noted for his piety and high moral values. He was clearly on top of the latest techniques for encouraging learning among the young boys in his charge, for Elwin took great care both to explain the Latin passage one boy was assigned to recite the next day and to repeatedly threaten him with a severe beating should he fail to do so to Elwin's satisfaction. The boy is not named, but the story's content and a quick scan of medieval saints' lives suggest that we might reasonably call him "Bartholomew," or "Bart," for short.

Off Elwin went to take up the other business of the day and so did young Bart. Unfortunately, for Bart this did not involve studying the passage or practicing its recitation. Instead, he was "seduced by his peers into playing games, and forgot both his teacher's recitation and his own lesson." Not good.

As the next day dawned, Bart was understandably freaked out. The flogging of schoolboys with bundles of birch branches—the symbol of the medieval schoolmaster in illuminations from the period—was something of the counter-Montessori philosophy of the day. The assumption behind these premodern approaches to education was that children were prone to lapse into sin at the slightest temptation. Medieval scholars worried, for example, that fables used in grammar instruction might encourage fabrication and falsification, and so they believed such takes should only be used when they served a clear moral purpose. The actual or threatened application of the rod was thought to be the best way to bring pupils into obedience. (This was believed to work well with wives, servants, beggars, and criminals in the Middle Ages, too.) The boy had every good reason, then, to fear the worst. Thus, "after much fretting and anguishing," Bart decided to hide out in the cathedral, where he could pray to one or another saint for protection and escape the ire of Master Elwin.

Not so fast! Elwin had been around the schoolhouse more than once, of course, and young Bart was not the first of Elwin's charges to skip class and hide out behind some dusty old tomb in the cathedral. The good master found Bart in no time, and dragged him back to the classroom, where he resolved to dole out two solid slaps of the birch each time the boy erred in his recitation of the lesson. That, surely, would teach him not to disobey.

Once again, not so fast. It seems that Bart had happened onto the tomb of St. Erkenwald, which, by all accounts, was quite grand. He no doubt thought it would be the perfect hiding place, but he also had the good sense to hedge his bet by prostrating himself on the grave and praying to the resting saint.

When Elwin discovered Bart and began dragging him back to the school, the boy grabbed onto a cloth that covered the tomb in an effort to resist. It didn't work immediately, but by the time Bart was back in the classroom staring down the barrel of Elwin's ill temper, St. Erkenwald's special spiritual powers had started to do their thing. Challenged by Master Elwin to recite the lesson, our slacker friend was able to go one better, repeating the lesson without error and adding, for good measure, the next lesson that had not yet been assigned.

But, wait—there's more! And this is where we get a deep insight into the habitus governing the medieval learning and culture in general. Elwin, as we might expect, was startled and awed by the miraculous spectacle, but also deeply ashamed. Why? Certainly not because he was about to pummel a prepubescent boy. Rather, Master Elwin "severely condemned himself," giving away all of his possessions to the poor and going into voluntary exile, because he saw in the miracle his failure to respect the authority of the saint and the effectiveness of the boy's intercessory prayer. He had, that is, failed in obedience just as young Bart had done by refusing to acknowledge the hierarchy that placed both him and the boy beneath the sainted bishop in the "natural" order of things.

Unlike his ne'er-do-well student, Master Elwin was fully formed in a habitus characterized not by the valuing of personal will—Bart's or his own—but by obedience reinforced by punishment or the threat thereof, more often than not in violent, physical form. So much had this commitment to obedience been reinforced in the medieval culture that it endured through the centuries over which this particular tale was transmitted orally before Canon Arcoid finally set it down in writing in the twelfth century. That is a durable habitus! So while Arcoid is sympathetic to Bart's fear of the impending beating, his criticism of the schoolmaster is reserved for Elwin's failure to "show a worthy reverence for God's saint" in dealing with the boy. In a no-pain-no-gain society like medieval England, it makes perfect sense that the teacher would send himself into exile from a community whose norms he has so clearly violated, depriving himself of any of the benefits that he drew from obedience to that habitus.

Why was regulated obedience so enduring through the Middle Ages? There are lots of reasons, of course. Religious beliefs in the period no doubt shored up the pervasive obedience to obedience. But we can't really blame religion on its own for the durability of the medieval adherence to the habitus of obedience. There were, after all, periods of dramatic climate change accompanied by flooding and drought, sundry plagues, the odd famine or two, and of course near-constant war-mongering. In such times, it's easy enough to understand why a broad commitment to obedience would seem like a good idea, even at the expense of personal freedom and cultural innovation. It should come as no surprise to us that change in such societies happens very slowly and innovation often appears to be more limited.

But we don't have to go back a thousand years to find this element of a habitus at work in a culture. Consider, for example, widespread American willingness to suspend a measure of personal freedom in exchange for the promise of greater security in the wake of the 9/11 attacks. We can only assume that much of what perplexes us in repressive societies today—Why do "those people" put up with *that*?—has to do with a habituated trade-off of a much more vague notion of personal freedom for a modicum of personal and familial security. Indeed, the word "faith" itself carries with it the promise of obedience in exchange for protection.

Nevertheless, we know that change does happen over time. Habitus shifts inch by inch, much of this marked out in stories like the Erkenwald tale. As we have seen, though Master Elwin is not singled out for pedagogical criticism in the tale, there is nonetheless great sympathy for the boy. "What can a boy do against a full-grown man, or the fearful against the furious?" Canon Arcoid wonders plaintively as he describes the schoolmaster angrily dragging his student from Erkenwald's tomb. Obedience to the habitus of obedience notwithstanding, here we see a kernel of recognition that the balance of power is out of whack in this situation.

Perhaps for centuries people wanted to challenge the prevailing habitus. Beyond the small hint in our tale, there is certainly a large volume of evidence that people were thinking about change and sometimes acting on these notions. The Robin Hood tales, for example, express a popular desire for social justice. And, from time to time there were local uprisings against unfair lords, the medieval Church hierarchy, and even princes and kings. Predictably enough, these were usually put down violently, thereby reinforcing the idea that disobedience is not such a good idea even if obedience isn't working out as well as we might like. "That's just the way of the world," ordinary people might have said, both acknowledging the durability of the prevailing habitus and ever so gently nudging it with passive critique.

In such an environment, the impulse to change is typically channeled though a higher authority rather than through outward dissent. "Justice" in the Erkenwald tale doesn't right the power imbalance between teacher and student directly. Bart, that is, does not develop his own sense of agency and challenge the cruelty of the teacher head-on. Rather, a greater authority is called upon to save the boy—the spiritual authority of the sainted bishop who, in turn, draws his power from God. The ultimate authority of God is so clearly understood that the saint does not himself punish the schoolmaster. That Elwin takes on himself, obedient to the end to the habitus of regulated obedience.

Still, the idea that there is something off in these kinds of relationships is clearly present, floating through cultural consciousness as one person tells the story to another over time and as Arcoid records it centuries later. It is a little thing, Arcoid's nod to the idea that a stern and proper beating is perhaps not always the best inducement to learning. It's barely half a tweet, in fact. And it would take nearly another millennium for the sentiment to be translated from Latin to English. But such gestures are rarely singular. Surely others were thinking that the grade school smackdown was getting a little old. And some of them were noting that idea in more permanent written documents that, over a much longer sweep of history, would contribute to a meaningful shift in the dominant habitus of Western Christendom. Indeed, in time the idea of regulated obedience as the core to learning and participating in society would undergo a revolutionary transformation. This new habitus—*a habitus of discovery and invention*—would endure up to the present day.

Revolutionary Diversions:
The Habitus of Discovery & Invention

In 1750, a couple decades before impudent protesters (if we take the British crown perspective) heaved chests of tea into Boston Harbor, a remarkable new book made its way from England to the American colonies. We cannot say precisely what formative effect the primer *The Child's New Play-Thing: being a Spelling Book Intended To make the Learning to Read a Diversion instead of a Task*[3] had in itself on the political actions of British Americans. But it cannot be denied that Mrs. Mary Cooper's now quite innocent-sounding book—"consisting of Scripture-Histories, Fables, Stories, Moral and Religious Precepts, Proverbs, Songs, Dialogues, etc."—was a carrier of a radical way of thinking about learning, literacy, and the nature of knowledge in general that would play a critical role in the American and French revolutions that shook imperial Europe by the time her book's target audience had come of age.

Directly or indirectly, the widow Cooper's approach to the education of children was influenced by the seventeenth-century British politician and philosopher John Locke (1632–1704), who was notable for his involvement in the Glorious Revolution of 1688, which restored England to Protestant rule under William III and Mary II and, some scholars argue, ushered in the Enlightenment. As a philosopher, Locke is remembered for his anti-authoritarian position with regard to personal freedom, the development of knowledge, and institutional legitimacy. A Puritan, Locke hardly recommended a freewheeling, experiential education for children. Still, he was insistent that, rather than being cowed, bullied, or beaten into conformity, children—"citizens in the making"—should be educated in ways that fostered the development of adult, independent reasoning capacity.

Against the pedagogical standard of discipline and obedience that we saw in the medieval Erkenwald tale, the idea that children might "discover" knowledge through silly-seeming alphabet games ("A, apple. B, bite it. C, cut it. D, divide it. E, eat it. . . .") was quite startling—revolutionary, even. For Mrs. Cooper's methods drew from Locke both a different understanding of the structuring of innate human consciousness than had previously been assumed and proposed practices for the development of knowledge and the capacity for reasoning that influenced the formation of moral character and norms for social behavior.

In this view, it is possible for a child to discover the Good that God intends through experience in the world created by God. But it may also happen that a child discovers wrong or even evil in the course of human experience. God does not exactly intend this. (Remember, we're assuming God has given people free will.) Rather, it is *permitted to happen* in the service of some Greater Good that we are not necessarily able to discern at the time. In the case of our medieval friend, Bart, for instance, it could be argued that the sin of disobeying the schoolmaster was permitted by God so that the greater good of both Bart and Elwin coming to an appreciation of the power of prayer and the authority of God through the saints could be realized. Or, it could also be that Bart's sin was permitted so that, centuries later while corporal punishment in school is still legal in twenty-two states, we might reflect on the practice of beating schoolchildren. Despite the risks, then, the process of discovery—including making mistakes—is considered essential to learning in a narrower content-based sense as well as in a wider moral sense.

Reading, Writing, & Revolution

The pedagogical method illustrated in the *Child's New Play-Thing* also participated in a related educational shift that brought together the intellectual practice of reading and the technical practice of writing, activities which had been understood as functionally distinct since ancient times. Until the modern era, to be "literate" meant only to have the ability to read—more particularly, the ability to read Latin. Writing was a craft practiced by scribes, not their masters—no more than understanding C++ or some other computer language today is a requirement of "computer literacy."[4] The craft of pre-modern writing was actually quite difficult, often very dirty work undertaken with rough materials and requiring painstaking attention. Literate men (and a few women) of station would hardly take up such a task.

However, the children Mrs. Cooper imagined discovering the letters and sounds of the alphabet and gathering them into phonetic readings of fanciful tales (with enhanced moral content for American audiences) were also invited into the craft of making letters and words themselves. Reading words is one thing; making them appear on a page yourself is entirely another. Remember when you had to pay a web designer or coerce someone's geeky cousin into creating even the most rudimentary web page for your church? Now you can do most of that yourself without the need for any technical training. Sure, professional web designers are generally more skilled than amateurs, just as professional writers are usually better than amateurs. But opening the field of technical and creative possibility to every child (or, in the eighteenth century, at least every boy of European descent from above the laboring classes) was truly huge in cultural terms. Rather than memorizing and repeating the words of "ancient masters" in order to base their thinking and acting in the world on "classic" knowledge, children o f the Enlightenment were actively encouraged to think up whole new ideas on the basis of their exploration of all of creation.

Further, while adults would certainly participate in this new approach to learning, their role was to guide children in developing *their own* reasoned reflection. This shift called into question things like the nature of authority, the development of personal and social identity, the status of tradition, and the essential character of Truth itself. Why, if children could simply *discover* knowledge, would they not have their own authority over it? What if they went about it the wrong way or came to incorrect or unorthodox conclusions? How would their errant thinking be checked? All of the worries that medieval churchmen had exercised over laypeople reading the Bible in languages they could understand came easily to mind again over the idea of giving children greater license to guide their own learning in general.

It is no small irony that over the next three decades, as Americans won independence from the British, a steady stream of educational and leisure reading imported from England was in essence contributing to the formation of an American mode of consciousness and decorum oriented toward personal freedom, exploration, and participation that challenged many long-standing sources of status and authority. In a fledgling country in which half of the white males were under the age of twenty, the significance of these new ways of accessing, structuring, and—with the melding of writing to reading in the new construction of literacy—creating knowledge cannot be underestimated. Continuing national mythologies related to "American ingenuity" and "know-how" have much to do with the shift in practices of presenting and accessing information, developing understanding, and creating knowledge represented by the *Child's New Play-Thing* and similar books. It is arguably the maturation of this very habitus of discovery and experimentation that, ultimately, yielded the explosion of technological, industrial, and cultural innovation in the twentieth century.

New American revolutionary fervor notwithstanding, not everyone agreed that learning should be so much child's play. The close association of learning with punishment or the threat thereof has had an enduring role in American education. Given this, the *Child's New Play-Thing* was more often found among household leisure books than in formal educational settings. There, more rigid, often punitive practices drawn from the Middle Ages continued to hold sway. Noah Webster, whose *American Spelling Book* (1836) was the dominant primer in American schools in the nineteenth century, took the view that education was meant to reinforce moral and civic values. His speller was long on memorization and repetition controlled by an educator whose unquestioned authority was backed by the smart *thwap* of a ruler across an errant child's knuckles. Not much fun at all.

Nevertheless, just as Arcoid's sympathy for the boy in the St. Erkenwald miracle tale sounded a subliminal note of concern, the popularity of children's books like the *Child's New Play-Thing* points to a crack in the durable structure of the medieval habitus of regulated obedience. Through the eighteenth and nineteenth centuries, richly illustrated children's books would themselves become clearly indentified artifacts of an emerging habitus of regulated discovery. Some scholars also suggest that these playful learning indulgences were the early seeds of the youth culture that developed more fully after World War II.

For those with affection for the certainties of an obedience-based culture, learning linked to the valuing of children's innate curiosity, inquisitiveness, creativity, and attraction to novelty would certainly have been unsettling. Indeed, those of us who sometimes struggle to understand how kids are communicating today with native fluency in email, text messaging, gaming, and other forms of digital media probably would not have difficulty sympathizing with the frustrations of our forebears who were caught in the transition from traditional medieval to newfangled Enlightenment ways of thinking, believing, and acting. "Now we're actually *recommending* that children read fables for *entertainment*?" they might have wondered in disbelief. If they'd added, "From there, it's a slippery slope . . ." they wouldn't have been far from wrong. We need only consider evolving practices of communication linked to children's play with words and their impact on the development of personal and social identity, notions of authority, and consequent reconfigurations of concepts of leadership and community that vex mainline churches today to see where "unregulated" curiosity can lead.

At the end of a long, productive era defined by a habitus of discovery and invention—one that grounded everything from the industrial revolution of the eighteenth century to the dot-com boom of the twentieth—we now find ourselves at the beginning of a new shift to a *habitus of regulated improvisation*. All of this started with the development of networked computing in the 1960s that would lead, by the 1970s—really, in a blink of historical time—to the creation of email and, in the 1980s, the formation of the internet. From there, it has been a quick leap to the interactive, mobile digital media that is underwriting changes throughout late modern culture, not least with regard to religious practices.

Pre-Texts of the Digital Reformation:
The Improvisational Habitus

To see something of this new habitus, let's fast-forward to a controversy in Scotland in 2003, when the National Association of School Masters and Union of Women Teachers called for a ban on the use of "txtspk," or "textspeak," the abbreviated language used for sending text messages and posting on digital social media sites such as Myspace, Facebook, and Twitter.[5] Here is part of an essay apparently submitted by a thirteen-year-old Scottish girl for her English class that captured the attention of news outlets across the globe:

> My smmr hols wr CWOT. B4, we usd 2 go 2 NY 2C my bro, his GF & thr 3 :-@ kds FTF. ILNY, its gr8.
>
> Bt my Ps wr so {:-/ BC o 9/11 tht they dcdd 2 stay in SCO & spnd 2wks up N.
>
> Up N, WUCIWUG - 0. I ws vvv brd in MON. 0 bt baas & ^^^^^.
>
> AAR8, my Ps wr :-) - they sd ICBW, & tht they wr ha-p 4 the pc&qt...IDTS!! I wntd 2 go hm ASAP, 2C my M8s again.
>
> 2day, I cam bk 2 skool. I feel v O:-) BC I hv dn all my hm wrk. Now its BAU

Translation (for the txtspk-impaired):

> My summer holidays were a complete waste of time. Before, we used to go to New York to see my brother, his girlfriend

and their three screaming kids face to face. I love New York; it's great.

But my parents were so worried because of the attack on September 11 that they decided we would stay in Scotland and spend two weeks up north.

Up north, what you see is what you get—nothing. I was very, very, very bored in the middle of nowhere. Nothing but sheep and mountains.

At any rate, my parents were happy. They said that it could be worse, and that they were happy with the peace and quiet. I don't think so! I wanted to go home as soon as possible, to see my mates again.

Today I came back to school. I feel very saintly because I have done all my homework. Now it's business as usual . . .

It's not clear whether the essay was an experiment on the part of the student or, indeed, a hoax by the teacher to make a point about declining standards of written English. And linguists are divided over whether it is, in fact, non-standard English inasmuch as, while unconventional in spelling, the essay's structure, syntax, and usage conform to standard grammatical rules. It is not, that is, wholly unregulated language use.

What is plain, however, is that this kind of playfulness with language generally drives adults nuts. It's one thing to use silly codes for secret summer camp conversations and entirely another matter to enter it into more formal settings meant for more serious endeavors—at least in the view of many educators, parents, and other keepers of linguistic correctness. Nonetheless, some linguists and educators see the use of txtspk as part of the natural development of language with which we are all going to have to come to grips eventually.

Regardless of where you might stand on this particular debate, we can see in the txtspk essay the shift in habitus that we are now experiencing—a shift from the regulated discovery of the modern age to a form of *regulated improvisation* that characterizes much of postmodern reality. While the idea of improvisation is unsettling to some, in the tale of the txtspk essay it is constrained by longstanding social conventions. It is regulated, and it is only against this regulation that the improvisation has any real meaning.

I've noted already that the essay is generally grammatically correct. Beyond that, assuming that the essay was in fact submitted by a student, she has conformed to the rules set by her teacher to write about her summer holiday. Indeed, she reports feeling "v O:-)" (very saintly) for having completed all her homework. Where she improvises, however, is not only in using the casual, abbreviated lexicon of the text message for her essay, but in asserting that this is appropriate for the classroom. There is perhaps a bit of a rhetorical flourish in this if we consider that the student is using what was likely her dominant vacation language to describe the vacation. She's letting the reader—her teacher—into the genre of texting that characterized her holiday communications, offering a winking intimacy into which teachers are not often invited. She is sharing something of the immediacy of the texting experience as an important element of her narrative. In this sense, she's actually quite a clever writer.

Beyond this, the student's sharing lays bare her preferred mode of communication with friends. While my school friends and I secreted away our wordplay from adults, the txtspk essayist is fully transparent, inviting her teacher into her world. The coda to her brief narration of the details of the holiday is an unspoken groan along the lines of, "And I only survived the tedium of it because I could text with my friends." The teacher is integrated into the experience through the student's use of the lexicon that recreates, in the essay, the normative use of digital technology for all manner of communication about the details—mundane or otherwise—of daily life. Her smartphone may be out of sight, but it is nonetheless present in the essay. It takes more than a dictionary of txtspk with which to translate the essay to get the full meaning. Only by grasping the nature of the technology as it functions in the context of kids' social lives can the essay really be understood.

In the tale of the txtspk essay, we see evidence of an important shift in the understanding of authority that is worlds away from the medieval hierarchical notion of authority to which obedience is owed. The student here does not turn to the teacher to authorize her improvisation; she assumes her own authority in doing so. The student understands that it is the teacher's role to assign, collect, and evaluate the homework, but in her use of txtspk, she nonetheless sets herself on parallel footing with the teacher.

If I am right in reading a rhetorical cleverness in the essay, it may also be that the student sees herself as responsible for entertaining and delighting her teacher. Certainly, the essay catches the teacher's attention enough to encourage her to put the essay into broader play by entering it into a developing viral news cycle. In doing so, the teacher herself acknowledges the significance of media in contemporary culture and claims her own authority as a "reporter" on educational matters. That the story quickly went globally viral only serves to reinforce this new digitally sponsored authority. Even as the teacher complains about the effects of the new habitus of regulated improvisation, she cannot help but participate in it.

Learning for the Reformation:
Some Characteristics of Digital Habitus

This small glimpse of a learning practice undertaken by a contemporary student—indeed, one largely driven by her—bears many of the hallmarks of a habitus of regulated improvisation that defines much of the habitus of the Digital Reformation:

- *Immediacy*—The essay mimics the "as it happens" quality of txtspk, and of digital communication more generally.
- *Transparency*—The essay easily offers the reader a glimpse into the daily life of the student.
- *Interactivity*—The model of texting that the student uses in the essay suggests the interpersonal, interactive quality that characterizes digital communication.
- *Co-Creativeness*—Along with interactivity comes the option for shared creativity. The essay's txtspk form invites the teacher to play along with her improvisation.
- *Integration*—The use of the txtspk genre for the class paper shows the student's assumption that digital technology and its norms are integrated into every aspect of life.
- *Distribution*—The teacher's response to the essay was to alert the media, extending a local conversation in a schoolhouse in Scotland across the globe and, even in her critique of the student's use of txtspk, participating in the digital communication practice used by the student.

The Overlapping Evolution of Habitus

We will explore these characteristics as they impact communication, leadership, and community in the context of mainline religion in the remaining chapters of *Tweet If You ♥ Jesus*. Before we do that, however, I would make one final note: It takes a long time for a habitus to be fully extinct. This is, in part, because generations overlap in any given time period. These days, generational overlap is much greater than in the past, with many families being composed of people from five generations. So, your great-grandmother may act out of lingering shards of the habitus of regulated obedience that her grandmother passed on to her. People who are now over fifty came of age at the height of the Atomic Age—a period of extended exploration and invention that surely shaped our approach to the world and spurred the development of the digital technologies that are reshaping our world today. That particular habitus influenced the life practices of the next generation even as they were forming a new habitus.

What constitutes a habitus, then, has much to do with the network of relationships that make up a particular community, the various forms of habitus that endure among those relations, and the creative play between them. At the local level, things are always a little murky, a little in flux. In the end, the process of change is never linear; it never progresses cleanly from one stage to the next. In the Middle Ages, the balance of shared cultural practices was oriented toward obedience. After the Enlightenment, in the modern period, the balance shifts:

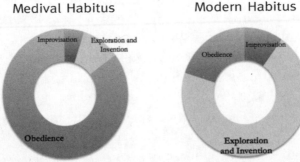

Medival Habitus   Modern Habitus

Improvisation Exploration and Invention   Improvisation

Obedience   Obedience

Exploration and Invention

Whereas the habitus characterizing the Digital Reformation might look more like this:

Digital Habitus

In religious contexts, habitus typically has a more lingering durability because contemporary religious practice is defined in response to the origins of the faith tradition in question. Roman Catholicism and Islam, for instance, retain much of the medieval habitus from which they developed. Obedience to religious authorities remains a core principle and practice. While in some extreme cases, violence to enforce obedience is given religious justification, in neither religious tradition are such practices any longer considered normative nor, in the case of Roman Catholicism, are they formally condoned. However, not long ago, members of a Roman Catholic congregation in Ohio were under threat of excommunication for failing to obey their bishop's decision that their parish church should be closed and the congregation integrated into other local parishes.[6] The congregation has apparently further piqued the ire of the bishop by insisting that he communicate not with the priest, following the traditional hierarchy, but with the new church community's organizing committee. All of this, according to the bishop, put the salvation of the whole community at risk. And so it goes.

Lutherans, Presbyterians, and Episcopalians carry remnants of the same medieval habitus, but their doctrines and practices are also defined by the controversies of the European Reformations that paralleled the Enlightenment's push into the modern age. They might well have been called, in their day, "postmedieval" (had people living in the Middle Ages thought of themselves as "medieval," that is). As global connectedness brings together local expressions of these early modern traditions—the worldwide Anglican Communion serves as a prime example—we see clashes that reflect differing degrees of durability and rates of change from one dominant habitus to another.

Other mainline traditions such as the Methodist, American Baptist, and Society of Friends (Quakers) churches developed in response to the larger Lutheran and English Reformations. More modern cultural practices and intellectual underpinnings mark the habitus that characterize them. The United Church of Christ and Christian Church (Disciples of Christ) traditions are products of a distinctly American experience of negotiating faith in the early life of a nation with expressed values of liberty, equality, and freedom. Evangelical and non-denominational churches developed out of the "Great Awakening" of the nineteenth century, and blossomed along with mass media platforms such as radio and television. The values of the Broadcast Age thus shape not just their use of media, but also their practice of church more generally.

Given the distinctiveness of various mainline religious traditions as they have developed in North America, the explorations we will take up of communication, leadership, and community in the Digital Reformation in the chapters ahead must be mapped to the particularities of denominational traditions and their local expressions. Where one mainline denomination is challenged by new distributed digital communication practices, another may be more vexed by the reconfiguration of authority and leadership that characterizes the Digital Reformation. Churches with remarkably strong traditions of developing vibrant, intimate, local communities within which leadership is more easily shared and transparency in communication is unproblematic may chafe at the wider, disembodied constructions of digital community.

Balancing Habitus in Your Community

One useful way to consider how your church can most productively engage the communication, community, and leadership practices of the Digital Reformation is to begin to articulate your own habitus.

What is the "rule of life" for your community against which the improvisations of life in the Digital Age take place? In your community, how would you assess the balance among qualities of obedience, exploration, invention, and improvisation? How would this assessment differ in the perspectives of longtime members, new members, younger adults, parents, singles, and so on? When you consider the integration of digital social media into the ministries of your community, what are your biggest fears with regard to how this might change your community? How might new social media challenge your own practices of ministry? Taking some time to assess "the way things go around here" in your particular world will go a long way toward helping you to bring the best qualities and most meaningful resources to engage the challenges ahead.

Part II

COMMUNICATION & THE DIGITAL REFORMATION

THE BOOK AS
COMMON PRAYER

Social Media Past & Present

Late medieval and early Renaissance connoisseurs, who mourned the loss of the scribal hand and pages that integrated words and images, considered printing a crude technology that destroyed aesthetic quality and blamed it for removing an important source of beauty from the world.

—*George P. Landow*

Periods of cultural change are often unsettling. But they can certainly be exciting, as well. When America took up the race to the moon, for instance, people around the world were inspired by the optimism and imagination of the lunar mission. The day astronauts from Apollo 11 landed on the moon—July 20, 1969—my family, along with a number of the neighbors, gathered in our living room to watch together on our hulking box of a console TV as Neil Armstrong made his "one giant leap for [hu]mankind." We merrily toasted one another with glasses of Tang, celebrating a season of adventure that, however briefly, drowned out daily casualty counts from the Vietnam War. In that moment, at least, uncertainty and fear were dominated by enthusiasm and hope—the marks of the modern habitus of discovery and invention fully realized.

I was a very small child at the time, so I can't say with any certainty exactly what I made of all this or how the grownups around me saw it. I know I liked the Tang a lot. I don't, in any case, recall the day having been marked with any sense that this remarkable accomplishment had changed everything. Its effects still seemed light years away from us. For most mainstream, middle-class Americans, it is probably fair to say that the moon landing solidified America's technological and political leadership in the world and may have helped to redeem that status from its darker applications in Hiroshima and Nagasaki a generation before. More than presaging a radical change in American life that would be underwritten by technological innovation almost at the speed of light, however, the Apollo mission seems to have reinforced an early modern idea of America that had long been changing. There we were, worshipping together at the altar of television as the modern mythology of American ingenuity and global prowess was visited upon our collective consciousness in the sanctuary of our own home. The very ritual in which we were all participating—a ritual replicated in millions of homes across America—might itself have signaled us that the times, they really were a-changin'.

Modern technologies—from the printing press to the television to the rocket ship to an ever-expanding array of engineered instant "foods"—would, by the time I was out of college, take us worlds away from much of the life we knew, tied as it was to our living room, our house, our little neighborhood, and the church up the street where almost everyone we knew worshipped on Sunday. Perhaps we should have seen it better then, but we don't always know when we're in an especially transitional time. So it was, I guess, that the moon landing quickly became the ironic punch line in a cliché about everything that *couldn't* be changed: "We can put a man on the moon, but we can't . . ."

In the twenty years between the launch of the first widely available television broadcasts in 1948 and that "small step" in 1969, electronic communication technology had already reshaped much of the ordinary American lifestyle. Yet the nature of broadcast television practice itself, following the well-worn path of broadcast radio, was particularly effective at shaping a mass vision of a country of peace and bounty where even the agitations of anti-war protestors and civil rights demonstrators could be muted by the authoritative interpretations of respected newsmen and the distractions of mainstream entertainment. Yes, social tensions had been stirred across the nation, but on TV, for the most part, they were balanced out by the wholesome humor of Red Skelton, the whacky shenanigans of Lucy and Ethel, and the steadfast assurances that things were really just fine offered by a line of innocently quirky families from Ralph and Alice Kramden to Mike and Carol Brady. And, of course, though we had lots of new gadgets, the boys of *Bonanza* and the sweetly cunning ladies of *Petticoat Junction* reminded us that Americans were always rugged frontiersmen (and women) at heart.

Religious fare was a part of the broadcast mix, too, bringing normative voices of faith—these being mainline Protestant, reflecting the dominant construction of "American religion" in the era—into our living rooms, initially in the form of live feeds from local church services. Indeed, the first religious radio broadcast took place just two months after Pittsburgh radio station KDKA launched the radio era by broadcasting election returns in 1920. Calvary Episcopal Church, not far from the studios of KDKA, was the site of the first broadcast church service on January, 2 1921. KDKA continued to broadcast Calvary's Sunday evening services through the early 1960s. In hindsight, it was a promising start for mainline Christianity in terms of engagement with new modes of communication, leadership, and community-making.

But in short order, the religious voice of broadcast radio developed a more Evangelical accent, animated by the success of programs like Aimee Semple McPherson's broadcasts from the Church of the Foursquare Gospel's state-of-the-art studio in Angelus Temple in Los Angeles. "The spirit of revival," as Sister Aimee announced before the first broadcast in February 1924, was "now on the air," and it more or less drowned out moderate, mainline religious voices on radio to the extent that when broadcast television came to the fore, it hardly occurred to mainline religious leaders to take part. Thus, in 1961, when conservative Evangelical preacher Pat Robertson launched the first Christian television station in Portsmouth,

Virginia, mainline Protestants noted it with little more than a condescending eye roll. Robertson's influential and often controversial
program, *The 700 Club*, has been broadcast since 1966, making it
one of the longest running programs of any variety, and enabling it
to serve as a platform for Robertson's theocratic vision for America
and his own unrealized aspirations for political office. Pretty much
no one saw that coming.

As Evangelical Protestants and a certain brand of conservative
Catholics developed widespread media ministries, mainline Protestant denominations receded into the background of American
media and, it has increasingly seemed, much of American life in general. Glimmering mega-churches bring all the vibrancy and pathos
of a studio-wrestling-meets-*America's Got Talent*-meets-*The Dr.
Phil Show* extravaganza to hundreds upon hundreds of gathered
worshipers each week. Millions of viewers watch television broadcasts and online streaming video feeds of services from jam-packed
"cathedrals," while the modest Methodist church down the block
calls it a good week if fifty people show up for a Sunday service.
About as close as mainline Protestantism has gotten to entering the
mainstream media landscape of late—outside of debates on the
roles of lesbians and gays in the Church or marriage equality—is
as the anonymous backdrop to a gospel-infused sequence on the
hit television series *Glee*.[1] Such uses of mainline church buildings
as props highlight the rise in what British sociologist Grace Davie
calls "vicarious religion."[2] Our church buildings stand for a version
of public morality and spiritual refuge that people don't quite want
to give up, but in which they really don't want to participate in any
structured, sustained capacity.

Because mainline leaders in ministry are still struggling to
catch up with, or at least emulate, the broadcast media successes
of Evangelical and non-denominational Protestants, we look in
this chapter at the evolution of mass print media (books, magazines, newspapers) and broadcast media (radio, television) as these
have been engaged by American religions. Our attention here will
be focused on the distinctive characteristics of social media before
the invention of the printing press—what scholars often call
"manuscript culture." We'll see in another story from the life of

St. Erkenwald an illustration of what has come to be broad social reading practices that have much to teach us about communication in the Digital Reformation.

Opening the Book, Again:
Social Media Practice Before the Printing Press

By this point in the Digital Age, commentators on new media have followed a reasonably predictable path to illustrate the impact of new communication media. From Clay Shirky (*Here Comes Everybody*; *Cognitive Surplus*), to Nicholas Carr (*The Shallows*), to Nick Bolton (*I Live in the Future & Here's How It Works*), the historical starting point for understanding the implications of digital social media has been fifteenth-century Europe, as the first mechanically produced books rolled off the Gutenberg press. Contemporary media commentators have picked up on an idea that has long grounded the reflections of religious studies scholars, armchair church historians, and ministers hoping to explain the popular roots of the European Reformations: Access to less expensive, less time-consuming, more productive printing technology allowed for more rapid spread of alternative religious ideas to more people and with less control by religious authorities.

The printing press, historians have long held, significantly democratized access to knowledge and the ability to express new and often controversial ideas, at the same time speeding the transmission of new religious thought within and across communities and, ultimately, around the globe. This allowed what would previously have been internal theological and ecclesiological debates of the sort that had arisen over and over again throughout Christendom, and that had been more or less effectively put to rest by Church authorities, to extend unimpeded into common conversation. The result, in conjunction with a number of other social forces, was not the slow drip, drip, drip of mistakes, accidents, and minor innovations that gradually reshape a dominant habitus, but a more radical revision in religious practice that changed the Church forever. The same was true in the fields of politics, science, literature, music, the visual arts, and so on, which likewise opened to myriad new ideas that could more easily be shared with others, thus changing prevailing attitudes, assumptions, ways of relating, and the everyday practices of life in general.

With good reason, then, commentators compare the rise of digital communication technologies to this revolutionary period in history, typically noting that innovations in printing and the associated access to learning met with their fair share of "this-will-rot-your-brain" critics, even among those who generally approved of the new ideas blossoming in various fields. But the comparison is not entirely accurate. Indeed, while printing did open the book of knowledge, as it were, to many people who would not previously have had access to the world of religious and academic ideas, it also closed the book on certain modes of relational communication that were a central mechanism not only for the sharing of knowledge in the ancient and medieval world, but for the nurturing of relationships within and across social categories.

As we will see, prior to the printing press, reading was a deeply social practice that drew on traditions of oral storytelling, which braided the recitation of a tale with its interpretation by the teller and the real-time response of an audience. The English monk Robert Mannyng included a warning in his fourteenth-century *Chronicle* that his book was not to be read out by "no disours . . . no seggers, no harpours"[3]—storytellers, minstrels, and musicians of the sort who would take liberties with his tale. The medieval mystic and pilgrim Margery Kempe, who dictated the first autobiography in English to a series of scribes, reported sharing her own wisdom with the priest friend who read "holy bokys" to her.[4] Such accounts make plain that premodern bookish encounters were not centered on didactic performances for passive listeners, but were fully interactive engagements that enlarged any given book into a much wider social "text." The story was not just *in* a book, but *all around it*, in the varied and often overlapping interactions among readers, listeners, tellers, and re-tellers of a tale, a history, a poem, a saint's life, a Biblical parable, and so on.

It is this very construct of social reading that grounds the ritual of Bible reading still practiced in most mainline churches. Our emersion in a late modern habitus largely adapted to the visual by broadcast media causes many of us to attend more fully to the performance of the reading as it is carried out through the personality of the reader and the liturgical choreography of the Sunday service. And we certainly don't openly comment on what we see or hear during the delivery of a sermon. But this practice of passive, performance-based consumption of the Word in community is a relatively recent innovation that, as we will see, has contributed to a more general disengagement of people from mainline worship communities.

As historian Elizabeth Eisenstein reminds us, "sermons had at one time been coupled with news about local and foreign affairs, real estate transactions, and other mundane matters," along with the birthdays and anniversaries that are still noted in some of our churches—this tradition perhaps lingering because no mass media forum was available for the sharing of such personal milestones until Facebook came on the scene. After printing, "news gathering and circulation were handled more effectively under lay auspices," and, we might add, well outside of church. The social division of communication labor allowed by the printing press contributed, according to Eisenstein, not only to the much sharper modern distinction between secular and religious worlds and the information they respectively offered people in their attempts to create meaning. It also contributed to "the weakening of local community ties" that for centuries had been centered in the church.[5]

Through the broadcast age, increased access to religious programming—televised church services, revivals, religious education, and news programs—has contributed to the phenomenon of "believing without belonging." The phrase, coined by Grace Davie, reflects the lingering belief in broad religious principles or spiritual ideologies, and, in many cases, a continued nominal identification with a particular denomination, along with declining membership and participation in local churches. While highlighting some of the benefits of religious television to local churches, Davie maintained that religious television presented "the extreme case of belief without belonging, for it seems to permit, encourage even, a rather self-indulgent form of armchair religiosity."[6] Whether or not we evaluate religious broadcasting quite so sharply, it is clear that the availability of options for personal religious engagement outside of face-to-face, interactive community continues the social disconnectedness that eventually developed in the aftermath of mechanized printing.

Medieval Multi-Tasking:
Seeing, Hearing & Sharing the Book in Community

This didn't, of course, happen all at once. Actually, long after the invention of the printing press, until quite late in the nineteenth century, reading was a quintessentially social medium—a communal affair with a group of hearers gathering around a reader to engage a book, letter, newspaper, or other written work. Reading together in this way encouraged not just intellectual or, in the case of religious writing, spiritual understanding, but also enhanced interpersonal relationships that contributed to the shared life of communities and, it would have gone without saying in the Christian world, their churches.

Add to this the fact that premodern books were very often not the single-author volumes familiar to us today. A manuscript binding might include a bit of Chaucer, perhaps something from the life of St. Bridget, and part of an almanac or a treatise on herbal remedies. We might say that before the advent of the printing press, books were "mash-ups"—gatherings of this-and-that that captured the interest of a book's patron with a logic that could often only be ferreted out on the basis of a deep understanding of the circumstances of her or his life.

Perhaps someone prayed to St. Bridget while sick in bed, waiting for the local wise woman to come up with a nice chamomile-and-something-mysterious tea. Maybe remembering a recent reading of Chaucer's racy romance, *Troilus and Criseyde*—the bestselling bodice-ripper of the fourteenth century—was a distraction from persistent tummy pains. Perhaps Sister Mary Whatsit over at Syon Abbey visited her sick friend, and so it seemed fitting to commission an illumination featuring her at prayer. Possibly all of this came together when the recovered friend decided to sponsor the construction of a book for donation to the learned Brigettine nuns, who had joined Mary Whatsit in prayer during the illness.

On the other hand, it could have been that the diverse contents of a particular volume all happened to be finished on the same day and bound together for the sake of convenience and cost-effectiveness, along with an illumination of Sister Mary Whatsit by that naughty Brother Austin, who harbored an inappropriate particular affection for the blameless nun. We cannot say, of course, but we can discern from the books and library catalogues we have from before the fifteenth century that premodern book users were relatively unburdened by the idea of sequential ordering. They did not have the same understanding of linear thought as "natural," or clearly defined authorship as "normal," that contributed to Enlightenment understandings of the "focused" mind of the solitary reader and later modern concerns over individually held "intellectual property rights."

Though many medieval books were richly illuminated, these images didn't necessarily illustrate the writing on the page or in the book overall in a direct way. The medieval books we admire so much today are distinguished by the remarkable visual images in the body of a text and in the margins that scholars have frequently compared to hyperlinked images on internet "pages." These "miniatures" in medieval books (so named not because they were small—often they were not—but because they used red ink, or vermillion, the Latin word for which is *minium*) did not generally function as illustrations of something *in* the written text but, as in the case of Sister Mary Whatsit, in reference to something *beyond* it.

The patron of the volume might be shown receiving the completed book or supervising its writing. Or, a scene related to a saint might accompany a biblical text read on that saint's day in the liturgical calendar without otherwise having anything to do with the scripture passage. Of particular delight to us today, much of the marginalia in illuminated books expressed the opinions and feelings of the illuminator about all manner of things—his demanding wife, the debauched monks in his neighborhood, or his own bacchanalian exploits. Making sense of the images in relation to the textual content of a book required more than a linear, intellectual understanding of The Facts. It required social insight gained from a life of engagement with the habitus from which the book emerged and into which it was offered. Literal readers of books, including the Bible, significantly flattened the process of interpretation after the Reformations, amping up the volume on the world created by the words on the printed page as they spoke to an individual reader, but muting the treble and bass of the worlds that prompted the moment of inscription and received its product. This literalizing impulse, along with the reduced expense of printing books without images, eventually all but erased the practice of illumination and silenced the voices of history, myth, and community that surrounded books in ancient, medieval, and early modern Christendom.

Reading the Writing on the Wall: Expanding the Social Text

What's more, this social mode of reading was hardly confined to books. The "texts" of the premodern world took various forms, making the construction of narratives an interpersonal, multi-media experience. Much of this centered on the physical structure of the local church. Indeed, at the time of Gregory the Great in the sixth century it was said that "churches are books for the unlettered"— the illiterate, that is. The idea here was that the plentiful statues, carvings, stained glass windows, wall paintings, and other visual fare in ancient and medieval churches offered illiterate believers a compendium of Bible stories, saints lives, and church history with which to nurture and sustain their faith.

Still, the stories suggested in church art are notoriously fragmentary and no more related to core Biblical or other religious teachings than those in illuminated manuscripts. And, of course, they varied tremendously from place to place. In some churches, images of Mary predominated. Sometimes this was the Madonna; sometimes a grieving Mary; sometimes a more regal Queen of Heaven. Often, all of the above. In other churches, a patron saint was featured more prominently. Christ's infancy, passion, and crucifixion were regularly depicted, but there was typically very slight representation of Old Testament stories beyond the tale of Adam and Eve and the serpent from Genesis 3. The lives of the saints were liberally mixed in with biblical images, either of which were apt to be linked visually to portraits, statues, or tombs of wealthy patrons.

Added to this are graffiti—words, but mainly drawings—that were regularly contributed by congregants of ancient and medieval churches as memorials, commentaries on local concerns, representations of village lore, or notices of coming events. For instance, the walls of St. Mary's Church in Aswell, an hour's drive north of London, are etched with graffiti mourning the ravages of the fourteenth-century plagues. At St. Bartholomew's in Gloucestershire a remarkably detailed mermaid, a spouting whale, and other figures are carved into stone walls and benches. At St. Nicholas Church in Oddington, also in the Cotswolds, a popular medieval anti-clerical motif—a fox in a Franciscan habit—is etched into a wall.

Both graffiti and more formal carvings also carried forward pre-Christian images and ideas, as for example in the famous Green Man carving at Norwich Cathedral on a folding seat ("misericord," or "mercy seat," which was made available to those who could not reasonably be expected to stand through the whole service— the infirm, the aged, pregnant women, and those of gentle birth). Together, these images participated in the shaping of richly contextualized stories of faith in community that were "read" by believers week upon week.

Music was also a particularly central feature of the worship experience, whether in the mass proper, in private devotions, or in chanted prayers that marked the hours of the day. Not merely something *performed* in church before a passive congregation, music was, according to liturgical music historian Walter Knowles, "a fact of medieval life." He continues, "From songs at planting and harvesting to processions on pilgrimage and between scenes of city-wide dramas, music in the Middle Ages was far more ubiquitous than the iPod and other MP3 players in our society." Along with words, images, and symbols, music-making was part of the multimedia experience of premodern common life and shared spiritual meaning-making that was gradually privatized by the mechanized hum of the printing press.

Making spiritual sense of the wealth of adornment that often confounds late modern visitors to premodern churches was thus a necessarily social activity. It required sufficient emersion in the dominant habitus to easily recognize local figures, revered saints, and holy people, and the symbols of their lore. Along with this, "reading the writing on the church wall" demanded a familiarity with basic Bible stories, the shape of the liturgy, and the calendar of the church year as it connected to the seasonal rhythms of nature and common labor, as well as an understanding of the flow of music in the service as it spilled into the rhythms of daily life. It didn't hurt that churches didn't have the pews we enjoy today. Medieval folk, therefore, tended to mill around the church, chatting with one another and sometimes playing games, until a scolding from the pulpit gathered their attention to the formal worship service.

Erkenwald & Folk Read the Pagan Past: Putting the Social in Medieval Media

This multi-media, social reading practice plays out in what is today the most well-known tale of St. Erkenwald,[7] the sainted bishop of London we met in the previous chapter, whose heavenly intervention saved a young schoolboy from the schoolmaster's rod. The tale has to do with Erkenwald's role in the redemption of a pagan judge who is found intact in a tomb unearthed by workers digging the foundation for what would become St. Paul's Cathedral. A rhythmic, alliterative poem written in the fourteenth century lays out the ancient mystery (*Who is this pagan and why has his body been preserved?*) and theological conundrum (*How can a virtuous non-Christian be saved?*) that are solved as much through St. Erkenwald's ability to pray the resting pagan into speech as through his virtue and compassion when he hears the judge's story.

The marvel of the poem, beyond the miracle of salvation effected by St. Erkenwald, is the way it depicts the coming together of all manner of folk from the surrounding community—workers and young farm lads, priests and scholars, lords of the manner, and politicians—to try to decipher the "runish writing" on the tomb. Together they seek to make sense of the fine clothing still intact on the body that indicate that the pagan was a person of stature, consult the records of the cathedral for the names of an ancient lord or king who might fit the bill, and consider the wisdom of the elders by way of identifying the body. All of this takes place before they bother to call upon the local ecclesial authority, Bishop Erkenwald.

When Erkenwald finally arrives, he quickly surveys the tomb before saying mass and appealing for God's assistance in solving the mystery. In the tale's first miracle, Erkenwald's prayer is answered, and the resting pagan is enabled to speak. From this, the townspeople learn that he was no ordinary lord of the manor, but rather an exceptionally virtuous judge. His wisdom and honor in mediating the most thorny disputes of his day awed all of those gathered around the tomb. They were all—including Erkenwald—deeply anguished over the apparent spiritual injustice of his having languished in purgatory for eons, unable to enjoy eternal rest.

So moved is Erkenwald himself by the judge's beautiful and tragic tale that he prays to God again for some solace for the virtuous pagan. This petition, in turn, moves the judge to profess faith in the God who inspired such compassion and devoted obedience. As he makes his confession, Erkenwald sheds a single tear that falls on the judge's forehead, effecting the baptism necessary for the judge to enter into eternal rest as a Christian.

Once the miracle of the judge's salvation is complete, his body and juridical finery turn to dust, and his tomb is sealed into the deepest foundation of the new cathedral. The pagan past is thus redeemed by the Christian present, and it silently grounds the future. The whole community worships together, processing out of the church into the village, bells peeling across the common where, given the season (Pentecost), a festival associated with spring planting (itself an echo of the pre-Christian past) was likely underway. In the end, the St. Erkenwald poem shows us an extensive social and spiritual reading project of a sort that we can imagine unfolding often on a smaller scale as people gathered in premodern churches and wove images, music, liturgies, gossip, Bible stories, sermons, and local lore into coherent narratives that sustained their life together.

As easier access to less expensive printed books grew, and literacy rates rose across classes and genders in the modern era, this social practice was all but lost outside of faint echoes found in kindergarten story hours and the occasional college seminar. Reading for moderns—and eventually listening to music—became private, solitary activities, connected to the experience of others only when we reported on what we read, heard, or saw, and how we liked it. Even that, for the most part, we eventually handed over to professional critics who, until very recently, had the last word on what was Good or Bad.

In our churches, the modernization of reading practice meant that personal engagement with sacred stories was disconnected from that of other believers. Oh, we might have various Bible study or book groups in church (and try to find someone under age thirty in one of those!), but these conversations are not part of the public, professionally regulated worship service. So marginalized have social reading practices become that many of the embodied qualities of reading—"voice," "tone," "interpretive communities"—have become merely metaphors applied to the written word.

The TV Is Disconnected:
Premodern & Modern Communication Practices

The arguably deleterious effect of the printing press on all this richly textured relational, imagistic, convergent, and participatory premodern media may seem galaxies away from the televised moon walk that captivated me and the folks of my little hamlet in 1969. But the printing press was more than a new technology. It was the technology of a new way of life—a whole new habitus that took shape, slowly at first, across Western culture, reaching its zenith perhaps just before the MTV moon man planted his own flag on the new frontier of American popular culture in 1981. Straight into the Broadcast Age it brought several communication features that have had a widespread impact on modern life up to the present day. Consider these in comparison to the characteristics of premodern social media:

PREMODERN SOCIAL COMMUNICATION	MODERN MASS COMMUNICATION
• Premodern social communication was based on face-to-face engagement between readers and hearers of a tale, poem, Bible passage, or other written text.	• Modern mass communication from the book to the newspaper to radio and television is a one-to-many proposition.
• Premodern social communication was fully interpersonal, interactive, and multi-directional, inviting presenters, consumers, and re-presenters of media (and often producers) into lively conversation.	• Modern mass communication is one-directional, moving from the owners of media outlets to consumers.
• Premodern listeners to written texts were quite active participants, encouraging or challenging writers and tale-tellers throughout the telling.	• The "mass" in the mass communication model are passive consumers of media products.
• The interactive format of premodern social media militated against anonymity.	• Consumers of broadcast media are, in the main, anonymous to one another.
• The authority of a text—knowing who created a tale—was so important to premodern readers that when they didn't know who created a particular text, they often added to the story by making an author up.	• Producers of broadcast media are, likewise, so removed from consumers as to be anonymous to them.
• Situated amongst producers and communities of listeners were entertaining readers, who encouraged interaction with the text.	• Situated between consumers and producers are larger-than-life, charismatic personalities who invite fantasies of connectedness.
• The measure of effectiveness with interactive, social media is further sociality, so interest is correlated to sharing or retelling the story.	• The measure of effectiveness in passive, consumer-oriented broadcast media is more consumption, so consumer interest is correlated to purchasing behavior.
• The way to impact sharing behavior is to offer captivating stories that can be adapted to local or personal interests by other tellers.	• The way to impact purchasing behavior is to offer captivating entertainment and then to interrupt it with a commercial message.

We will explore the profound impact of these communication practices on communities in Part III, but with regard to communication practice itself, there is of course a significant overlap inasmuch as premodern communication—not unlike communication in the Digital Reformation—is fundamentally grounded in creating and sustaining relationships. Communication practices based on privatized acts of creativity that are hidden behind the curtains of so many broadcast media wizards who reveal their dazzling messages to consumers increasingly fall flat on late modern believers, who value transparency, authenticity, and collaboration. In this way, believers and seekers in the Digital Reformation have much more in common with our premodern ancestors.

This means that the slickest video you might produce for YouTube is often going to fail against Father Matthew's dorky, self-produced lessons with monkey puppets, bad music, and Dixie cups. It's why Betty Butterfield's campy evaluations of various Christian denominations get more hits than any mainline denominational video.[8] The measure of effectiveness for these amateur video series is the tremendous amount of conversation they generate in social media settings, both on YouTube itself and through routine sharing on Facebook and Twitter. Beyond this, both have encouraged other amateur religious videographers to share their own perspectives on the Church, its gifts, and various foibles. These amateur creations share informational, spiritual, theological, and other content. But, like the pagan judge's elaborate tomb, the media through which this content is shared itself encourages a more significant practice of interactive engagement that has profound spiritual and ecclesial implications.

———

Because of this interactive priority in communications practices for the Digital Reformation, the road many leaders in ministry take into the social media landscape—the blog—can also be ineffective to the extent that it often winds through the glittering byways of your very best sermon without bothering to stop for a chat with the locals. When you consider the ways that you use both traditional media and new media to connect with, encourage, and extend your community, how much interaction and collaboration are you inviting? Take a long look at your newsletters, email blasts, and Facebook page, as well as the announcement section of your Sunday service or coffee hour. How have you invited participation through traditional and new media? To what extent do you see your communication practices—individually and in your community as a whole—as oriented toward building relationships and further sharing? How might you make communication a more social phenomenon in every aspect of your common life?

As we move more squarely into the heart of the Digital Reformation, it can be helpful to recall that our history holds many of the templates for collaborative, relational communication practices grounded in a faithful context. We don't, that is, have to start from scratch. In the next chapter, then, we'll take a spin through the back roads of the ancient Near East, as St. Paul made the most of the social media of his day to communicate with newly forming Church communities.

4

PARATWEESIS

Communication Practices for the Digital Reformation

I believe that being requires the other . . .

—*Linda Gregg*

When we're talking about technology, we naturally tend to think that the way to address the interpersonal, cultural, social, or spiritual issues about which we're concerned is through technology itself. So, when I talk with lay leaders and clergy throughout mainline churches, they often ask me about whether to use social media tools like HootSuite (which coordinates status updates across multiple social media sites) or Foursquare (which uses digital tracking to let people in your social networks know where you are), or what online video platform I recommend. But, surprising though this may seem in a book about digital media and religion, I'm here to tell you that *technology is not the answer*. Now, it's not the problem either. It just is what it is: the reality of much human relatedness in today's world. We have to engage it. Getting the right technology is not going to save our churches from irrelevance and oblivion. But engaging in communication practices that are appropriate to a world shaped by digital social media just might. The Digital Reformation is about orthopraxis—right practice—not orthotechnology.

Mary Hess, a professor of educational leadership at Luther Seminary, offers a powerful metaphor that allows us to see digital social media in ways that connect more clearly to our practice as Christians. Rather than seeing electronic media as "technology that enables communication"—a standard functional definition—or even in a perhaps more sophisticated way as "socially embedded sites for the ongoing negotiation of meaning as such,"[1] Hess encourages us to apply a biological metaphor. She understands "media," or "a medium," in the way biologists do, as "a culture in which to grow meaning."[2] In this light, a digital social medium becomes a site for growth, for creative engagement, cross-pollination, the evolution of the self, the community, and the Church.

When we think of a medium in this fertile way, our success in engaging it has not so much to do with our mastery of technology, but with practices of attentiveness, nurturance, and cultivation. Sure, there are some technical things we need to understand to steer the plow around the field, as it were. But seeing media as sites for creative growth in our communication with others encourages a focus on practices of spiritual care that are rooted deeply in our traditions. Moreover, such a practice-oriented view presses us to look beyond the personality-based models of communication that defined the Broadcast Age.

To put it another way, a carrot doesn't care how cool you are or how tricked out your spade is when you put seeds in the ground. It cares that you know it's a carrot and not something else, so you'll understand its particular needs for light, water, nutrients, and the space to grow untroubled by vermin. Among the things that can make the social media presence of churches and religious organizations effective today are practices that make it very clear that what these communities have to say—more often to ask, or to invite—has nothing to do with any particular individual per se. (Indeed, even Jesus—the second person of the Trinity—isn't about individuals.) It's all about tilling the soil, feeding the roots, maybe weeding a bit and playing music to encourage growth. The Digital Reformation demands such ministries of presence, encouragement, and, above all, abundant attentiveness to others.

Now, it seems to me that this is very good news for Christians in general, and for mainline Christians in particular, given the deep reserve of resources in our tradition that help us to encourage cross-pollination, creativity, and growth. Certainly, Jesus was into these sorts of practices, sullying his ministry in the minds of some of his contemporaries by trafficking with various and sundry lowlifes and listening to their stories, even as he unfolded God's story of love, justice, and hope. Out there "fishing for people" and "gathering in the harvest," Jesus recognized that the social media of his day—conversations, sermons, stories—were active mediums for the transformation of lives and the redemption of humanity. It makes me wonder exactly what Jesus might tweet were he walking among us today.

But the "what" isn't really so much the point, either. Or, at least it's not the starting point for engaged communication through digital social media. Indeed, part of the problem of bringing broadcast media practices into social media contexts is that they're all about the "what." Messages drive practice of communication rather than relationships. Meaning precedes interaction rather than growing from it. That's not the way it is in the Digital Reformation. Moving into the Digital Reformation, communication practices build on the premodern social practices and modern broadcast practices discussed in Chapter 3:

PREMODERN COMMUNICATION	MODERN MASS MEDIA COMMUNICATION	DIGITAL SOCIAL MEDIA COMMUNICATION
• One-to-group	• One-to-many	• One-to-one-to-one-to-two-to-fifty-to-three-to-five-thousand-to-two-to-one-to-nineteen . . .
• Whoever is here is enough	• More is better	• Less is enriched by more participation
• Interpersonal, multi-directional	• One-directional, top-down	• Multi-directional, networked
• Active, creative participants	• Passive consumers	• Active, creative participants
• Interactive producers, readers, and listeners	• Anonymous consumers and producers	• Interactive producers and redistributors
• Communication is mediated by enter-taining readers, who encourage interaction with the text	• Communication is mediated by charis-matic personalities who invite fantasies of connectedness	• Communication is facilitated by whoever creates or distributes a compelling idea that connects people to others on- and offline
• Participant interest is correlated to further sociality—success is measured by how much people share and retell the story	• Consumer interest is correlated to purchasing behavior—success is measured by how much people buy *after* receiving a message	• Participant inter-est is correlated to distribution—success is indicated by how much people share and elaborate *as* they are receiving a message
• The way to impact sharing is to offer captivating stories that can be adapted	• The way to impact purchasing behavior is to offer captivating entertainment and then to interrupt it with a commercial message	• The way to impact par-ticipation is by develop-ing engaging content, effectively sharing it with others, and invit-ing them to comment and collaborate
• The story itself, sur-rounded by the images and music of the community, encourage participative attention	• Flash, sizzle, and pop capture consumers' attention	• Flash, sizzle, and pop distract participants from meaningful con-tent and conversation

What this comparison illustrates is that changes in technology insist on changes in how we relate to one another. Our attention, then, needs not to be so much on the latest app or iPad upgrade the folks over at the technology news site *Mashable* are extolling. Rather, we need to focus on the very basic practices of Digital Age interpersonal communication that make our investment in such technologies worthwhile because they enable us to further share the Gospel of love and justice in the world.

In this chapter, then, we're going to focus more on the "how" of effective communication for the Digital Reformation by looking at some exemplary practices in the ancient Christian tradition that can help us to shape our engagement with new digital social media. In particular, we'll look at the Apostle Paul to learn about what we might call a proto-digital practice of blogging that speaks to digital social communications in a variety of formats. Then, we'll take a closer look at how creative leaders in ministry are in effect adapting these practices to spiritual life in the Digital Reformation.

Paul, Apostolic Proto-Blogger: Communicating Community in the Early Church

As with many well-known leaders, especially one so profoundly engaged in defining the communities that would in fact become the Christian church and the theologies that would animate them, we tend to think of "who" and "what" when we think of the Apostle Paul, rather than "how." Most people—scholars and academic laypeople alike—have focused on filling in the blanks in Paul's personal biography or clarifying his theological positions, the former typically in service of the latter. This is all to the good, but it does leave out of the picture the "how" of Paul's letter-writing ministry—a potential resource for practices of communication, as well as leadership and community formation, that are tailor-made for the Digital Reformation. To get at this, we have to set aside the larger-than-life convert, evangelist, martyr, and saint, and his immanently practical theologies, so we can see something of how he went about encouraging spiritual health among the early Christian churches through the comparatively limited, but nonetheless quite rich, communication media available in the first century Near East.

With this in mind, three things are important about Paul's letters. The first has to do with the construction of the letters themselves, which drew upon and adapted a wide variety of available linguistic, formal, and imagistic resources. The second concerns the communities to which the letters were addressed, each of which faced distinctive challenges as they attempted to live out a faith that marginalized them within the wider Greco-Roman culture. The third involves the means of distribution of the letters throughout the ancient Church, which modeled a kind of diverse, participatory Christianity that is as relevant today as it was in the first century.

The Pauline Mash-Up:
Making Pre-Digital Sense of Pauline Epistles

Though Paul made use of many of the formats and content sources for letter-writing in antiquity, he put them together in novel ways. Ancient business letters, love letters, letters of friendship, letters of introduction and advice, recommendation letters, discursive letters (speeches), and so on all had standard formats and relied on certain conventions that signaled the letter writer's understanding of and conformance to the norms of civil society. Paul knew all that, but he nonetheless felt free to play around the conventions. "Grace to you and peace from God our Father and the Lord Jesus Christ," Paul says in a greeting to the Corinthians (1 Corinthians 1:3) that is echoed throughout the epistles to the extent that we might read it is as something of a cliché. Not so much.

If we were living in Corinth in the middle of the first century, we would know that Paul was riffing on the standard Greek salutation *chairein* ("greetings") with the theologically freighted *charis* ("grace") while at the same time suggesting the Jewish greeting "Shalom" by offering "peace" to his readers.[3] In just about half the space of a tweet—seventy-eight characters—Paul manages to address the traditions of both Gentiles and Jews who will hear his letter read, while at the same time commanding and implicitly dismissing the Hellenistic rhetorical convention. He plays with language in a way that allows him to bridge an ethnic divide that would have seemed impossible in strictly social terms. In doing so, he gives the Corinthians language for a common faith without erasing their ethnic distinctiveness.

But he doesn't stop there. Paul is a master of the mash-up in content as well as in form and language. His letters are full of material from Jewish scriptures and the Gospels, of course, but also from Stoic and pagan writings. He quotes hymns and prayers, throws in lists of vices and virtues, and spices it up with images from domestic life, daily work, and sports. Like so many Harry Potter fans whose attachment to an amazing story drives them to create, collaborate, and share in order to enlarge the story—copyrights be damned!—Paul cobbles together whatever he finds among the available cultural resources to tell a story he believes transcends worldly cultural conventions.

The Plural Who: Attending to Early Christian Communities

Paul is more than a canny wordsmith in his letters, however, and it is here that we come to the second important point about Paul's letters for our purposes. As booming as his own voice is, there is another "who" that is equally significant in the letters—a "Plural Who" marked by the names of individuals, factions, and communities that amble in and around Paul's letters. There are his co-senders, and perhaps co-writers, among them: Sosthenes, Timothy, the elders and deacons of Philippi, and Silvanus. There are those included in the shout-outs at the end of most of the letters, including: Gius, Terius, Mary, Ampliatus, Urban, Stachys, Apelles, Phoebe, Apollos, Olympas, Julia, Philologus, Hermas, Hermes, Stephanas, Fortunatus, Achaicus, Aquila, Prisca, Euodia, Syntyche, Syzgus, Tychicus, Clement, and Barnabas. His prison-mates, Andronicus, Junias, Aristarchus, Mark, Jesus Justus; and supporters, Epaphras and Luke. Some twenty-six names are included in the epilogue to Romans alone.

Add to the above incomplete list a "loyal companion," a cluster of co-workers, and a whole host of souls "whose names are in the book of life" (Philippians 4:3) but not in Paul's letters, and we have a wide communion of saints with whom Paul is in conversation. But the Plural Who extends beyond those named or suggested as individuals in the text. The Plural Who is almost always the whole community—the whole Christian church—so the literal "you" Paul speaks to in the letters is nearly always plural. His scolding of the Corinthians plays a neat grammatical trick in this regard. "Do you not know that your bodies are members of Christ himself," is a typical modern English translation of 1 Corinthians 6:15. But the Greek is more subtle here. The "you" is plural, but "bodies" is singular. The conversation for Paul is always at once distributed among, and inclusive of, the whole community.

Moreover, the evidence of this distributed conversation is not limited to the letters we have. Rather, it extended to additional letters he alludes to that are no longer available to us, as well as a number of face-to-face visits back and forth between envoys of the new churches, Paul's representatives, and Paul himself. While many scholars rightly highlight the intertextuality of Paul's writings, it is no less important that he is a profoundly interpersonal communicator, whose letters address the active concerns of those with whom he is in relationship. Clearly, Paul was what we might refer to today as "a networked communicator."[4] This networked spirituality and ecclesiology is not merely context—something that surrounds the "real" Paul and his "true" message like so many planets surrounding one bright sun—but rather the core of a way of communicating and leading that depends on listening, engaging, and responding on the basis of a considered understanding of the concerns of others.

Thus, when we find Paul in his letters, we find him in the midst of conversation, in a world of people whose lives have been, on the one hand, utterly transformed by their faith in Jesus Christ and who, on the other hand, remain located in their ancient communities, roiled as they are by external oppressions as well as by internal bickering and spiritual backsliding. It is this reality that Paul's letters address, and when we read Paul now we do well to attend at least as much to what he was *hearing* from this Plural Who as to what he was *saying* to them.

By the time we encounter the Paul of his letters, remember, he has already preached the Gospel to the new Christian communities.

This is the story of much of the book of Acts. It is a given in his letters, which are pastoral rather than evangelical, that the Gospel was embraced (however much new believers waffled after Paul set sail to the next city). The encouragement, consolation, correction, solace, admonishment, and instruction—the *paraklesis* that Paul offers the diverse, far-flung Christians in his spiritual care—all of these are anchored not to Paul's perspective alone, but to the concerns of the people to whom he is writing. His theological understanding is shaped by their lived experience of faith—petty and venial though that experience often seems in the early Church communities—as much as it is by Paul's own experience of conversion, witness, welcome, conflict, and persecution.

Knitting the Body:
Collaborative Communication in the Pauline Churches

The spiritual reciprocity between Paul and the Christian communities with whom he corresponds is embodied as well in the ways in which the letters were transmitted and shared, both by way of conventional ancient practice and through Paul's own instruction to the recipients. This is the third significant point about Paul's communication practices as they might help us in the Digital Reformation. The very practice of creating the letters—the deep listening they required, the thoughtful reflection, the gathering of diverse formal, linguistic and imagistic resources, and, not least, the acts of writing, sending, receiving, reading, and distributing them—all of this enacted the community within which and to which Paul's letters spoke.

We've looked some at the many named and unnamed people mentioned by Paul in his letters. Some of these may have been co-writers. Others, such as the secretary Tertius who greets the Romans along with Paul and Gaius (Romans 16:22), may or may not have had a hand in shaping the contents of the letters. But the text itself is not the beginning and end of the collaborative, participatory practice that surrounds Paul's letters.

Getting a letter from, for example, Ephesus (in present-day Turkey) to Corinth (in present-day Greece) was no small undertaking. Travelling by sea from Ephesus, and then walking from the port, a very fortunate traveler could have carried a letter in about a week.[5] But getting there was only part of the picture. The trip would also have been expensive, especially for a band of travelling evangelists struggling to earn enough to keep body and soul together through irregular craftwork and the generosity of new converts. When Timothy carried a letter for Paul, he would have had to purchase food for the journey and fare for a ship across the Aegean Sea along with provisions for the two-day trek from the port to Corinth. Pulling such a trip together would have required the support of a number of people who went well beyond the ancient equivalent of clicking the "like" button. Folks actually had to pony up emotional, intellectual, and material support. Such efforts certainly gave everyone involved a personal stake in Paul's ongoing conversations.

The specifics of this collaboration are obviously not the same as would be needed for distributed communication today. Nevertheless, they point to a social embodiment of relationship- and meaning-making that continues to have important implications in the Digital Reformation. They suggest forms of collaborative ministry that have not yet moved from face-to-face practice to digital practice in particularly intentional ways. Sharing news and opinions, offering compassion and encouragement, celebrating life transitions, and gathering for brainstorming or problem-solving are all things that *everyone* in a community of faith can do online—not just clergy or formally commissioned lay leaders.

For Paul, sharing the Word went well beyond the writing and delivery of the letters. The letters were not merely the concretizing of conversations between Paul and a particular individual, or even a particular community. Paul "commands" that his letter to the Christians in Thessalonica be read in all the churches (1 Thessalonians 5:27), and he encourages the Colossians to swap letters with the folks in Laodicea (Colossians 4:16). All of this common reading and exchange would certainly have encouraged local interpretations of Paul's intentions, bringing the voices of other believers into the early understanding of Christianity and the practice of Church. Perhaps we would have a less messy, conflict-riddled Church if Paul had simply handed out standardized operating manuals to the early Church communities. But it wouldn't be *our* church; it would be *his*.

Beyond Blogging: Communicating Transformation

So, here is the "how" of it—a "how" that makes Paul a better proto-blogger than many of us who joyfully post our latest sermon on LiveJournal or WordPress. This is hard to believe, what with his frequent blustering about the authority he claims through Christ directly, but Paul turns out to be not so much about Paul. "Was Paul crucified for you? Or were you baptized in the name of Paul?" (1 Corinthians 1:13–14), he more or less spits at the errant Corinthians. Paul responds directly to what is happening in the community. This is what a good blog does: it responds to something *out there* rather than just expressing something *in here*. It's not about sending out a message, but about connecting to a lived reality and inviting people to share their own take on that. Good blogs feed conversations, which is why their measure of success is not how many subscribers they have—ego-gratifying though that might be—but how extensively they are distributed and redistributed, cited and even purloined.

Paul understood that the radically transformative power of the Gospel was so significant that he couldn't rely on a narrow view of the conventions of the existing media or the long-held hierarchies of communication. In a worldview premised on the radical idea that "there is no longer Jew or Greek, there is no longer slave or free, there is no longer male and female; for all of you are one in Christ Jesus" (Galatians 3:28), Paul had a keen appreciation of the fact that his strongest voice was everyone's voice, his most authoritative words were those that encouraged everyone into community and conversation. Of course, by his own frequent admission, he wasn't perfect. He didn't always get it right. That's okay to the extent that we're *still* in a conversation about how to make Christian community work—talking, tweeting and retweeting, sharing on Facebook, blogging, and so on about what the Gospels teach, or Paul might have meant, and what that means for us now. So, maybe it turns out that the pursuit of perfection isn't as important to the life of the church as the pursuit of the good conversation, precisely because it feeds relationship, and that grows community, which in turn encourages a more expansive social and ecclesiological wholeness.

Participating in the blogosphere—and in the social media landscape more generally—as a conversation generator and partner rather than as a digitized religious authority allows leaders in ministry today to engage believers and seekers exactly where they share many of their own concerns, hopes, interests, and questions. My hunch is that Paul would be just fine if your next blog post were less about his letter to the Philippians and more about what you've heard lately on Facebook and Twitter about how people are understanding their faith.

In fact, the irresistible impulse that many of us have to turn a blog post into an electronic pulpit, church newsletter, or other more formalized expression of religion is part of a general institutionalizing trend that is all but choking the life out of the once vibrant blog genre. Mainline Christian bloggers have the opportunity to infuse the form with new life by entering it as reflective listeners rather than as preachers. Beyond this, social media platforms like Facebook and YouTube allow leaders in ministry today to enact the kinds of co-creativeness and shared commitment to distributing the Gospel that characterized communication in the early Church communities, but in the real-time formats that are more congenial to believers and seekers today.

Blog You Later: Balancing Modes of Digital Engagement

It's easy to see how Paul's letters are a bit like blogs. But the lesson Paul offers today is that we communicate, lead, and encourage community most effectively when we make use of the most relevant formats for engagement. In his day, that was the letter. In ours, although the blog is a valuable supplementary format for more extended reflection, shorter posts on sites like Facebook and Twitter are often more engaging. The well-known religious writer Diana Butler Bass, for example, shares her thinking on contemporary religious issues through mass-media digital outlets like the *Huffington Post* or *Beliefnet*, but her Facebook page functions more like a digital salon where people gather to discuss Bass's brief comments on everything from church politics to economic justice to the antics of the family dog, Rowan. Bass uses her status as a "thought leader" in progressive, mainline Christianity to invite others into conversation, and their posts consistently extend well beyond whatever her originating comment might have been.

In fact, the progression and continuing interaction among social media formats is not unlike that found in face-to-face engagements. Twitter, for instance, is a bit like a public coffee hour. When you're at your best, you spend a little time with everyone, and take care especially to welcome newcomers. And, as at coffee hour, it's generally considered rude when a group of more established friends hangs out in a clique, telling inside jokes that highlight how much everyone else is *not* part of their set. Facebook, by contrast, is more like going to coffee with a select group of friends who might bring some of their own friends along. The conversation is still relatively public, and you might run into folks at the coffee shop who join in the conversation. A blog, however, is a poetry reading. Sure, it's public in a way. But it's pretty likely that only those people who already know you will come to hear what you have to say. If they like it, they might invite friends to the next one, or they might hang out afterwards to comment on your work.

The thing is, it's not likely that you would introduce yourself to someone and then immediately invite them to your upcoming poetry reading. You might mention that you write poetry in the context of a coffee hour getting-to-know-you or just-checking-in conversation. If there's a mutual interest, you might even go for coffee with other poetry-loving friends. All of this would happen before you started inviting people to your readings by way of creating a context for that invitation that comes off as something more relational than narcissistic.

In the same way, your initial and, I would argue, your most extensive social media engagements should probably be on Facebook and Twitter. We have Paul's letters both because Paul was Paul, and because there was no way to capture the ancient equivalent of what have to have been a tremendous number of coffee hour and café conversations with smaller subsets of early Christian communities. Pound for ecclesial pound, these smaller social networking occasions likely outweighed the letters in the formation of the Church. Similarly limited, other-focused interactions are at the center of the current reformation of the Church.

Status Update from the Church in the Digital World: How Social Media Are Revitalizing Church Communication

A number of religiously themed Facebook groups developed by less well-known leaders in ministry today have begun to undertake this sort of participative communication quite effectively. This is, of course, the beauty of Digital Reformation: anyone can have a go at facilitating regardless of their professional experience or status. Three Episcopal priests, for example—Susan Russell of All Saints Church in Pasadena, California; Ron Pogue of Church of the Good Shepherd in Lexington, Kentucky; and Chris Yaw of St. David's Church in Southfield, Michigan—have used Facebook pages for social justice advocacy, to develop a wider appreciation of the meaning of the Episcopal Church in the lives of members and friends across North America and the world, and to encourage the sharing of resources for ministry across local Episcopal communities. All three also use the longer blog form to express more extensive reflections. Both Russell and Yaw also have Twitter feeds. And Yaw has developed a video series that introduces the basics of Episcopal Christian practice. But their interaction on Facebook represents an evolution of Pauline communication practices that is particularly effective for life in the Digital Reformation.

Russell, for instance, created the "Anglicans Who Want THIS Statement from Canterbury" page, which includes some six thousand people who appealed to the archbishop of Canterbury to formally condemn proposed legislation in Uganda that would make homosexuality punishable by death. Participants on the page share news and information about the legislation and the responses to it in Uganda and around the world, including in their local congregations. Serving in a congregation with a long tradition of social activism, Russell sees social media as an integral part of her ministry and the Church's outreach to the wider world. "I'm fascinated by the opportunities provided by these new tools to proclaim the Gospel in the midst of people's daily lives rather than as a kind of performance in the Sunday service. I could preach about these issues—and I do—but Facebook pages like this bring more people into the story, so it's *our* story, *our* message." She adds, "I'm just convinced that if Jesus were with us today, he'd be blogging, tweeting, and posting on Facebook."

Both Pogue and Yaw have used Facebook pages in less topical ways, focusing more on the wider development of Episcopal community. Yaw developed the "People Who Are Rather Fond of the Episcopal Church" page in early 2009 to engage people who identified denominationally as Episcopalian and non-Episcopalians, and to celebrate the diverse ministries of local churches and their positive impact in the lives of people and in communities. "As leaders in the Church, we have to be thinking about the big picture," Yaw insists. "We have to be thinking about how we unite more than just my local community, about how we can be a force for good in the diocese, and in the world beyond that." His development of the group page was aimed at linking the many individuals and churches he saw on Facebook so that people could "engage in a communal appreciation of our Episcopal heritage." In response to a question that Yaw messages to the three thousand or so group members each month, participants share stories, images, and other resources that show "what we're rather proud of today in our church."

This isn't just so many Episcopalians "raising the banners high" for the sake of self-congratulation. Like early church communities, most mainline church communities today are small. According to the Duke University National Congregations Study, the average mainline Protestant church has a weekly attendance of about seventy-five people.[6] Yaw sees this smallness as a particular virtue of mainline churches in a world full of "big box" Christianity. But he also sees the same necessity for communication among these small communities that concerned Paul. "We have communities without rectors, communities sharing priests, communities coming together to worship without the full complement of resources that they might see as ideal," he explains. Yaw continues:

> With the strides in communication we've had over the last several years, our communities can really be a lot bigger in very

meaningful, practical ways without losing the value of smallness. People are really helping each other with the exchange of ideas, stories, and just simple connectedness with people who are alike in important ways. I think this helps these smaller churches to see themselves as an important part of the whole communion, and that's incredibly important.

The Facebook group created by Pogue, "Unapologetically Episcopalian," has similar aims, but goes at them in a somewhat different way. Like Yaw, Pogue felt that the tone of conversation across the Episcopal Church and in religions more generally had become overwhelmingly negative. "I just felt that we were doing too much apologizing and not enough celebrating of what Episcopalians have been doing in sixteen nations to spread the Gospel," he says. "The vast and vital center of the church has been working incredibly hard over the years to get on with the mission of Christ, but their voices have been drowned out by the extremes within and outside the church."

On May Day 2010 (no kidding), after getting one more late-night email complaining about something else that was wrong in the church, Pogue decided to create a Facebook group page dedicated to sharing the reality of positive, meaningful Christian community in the Episcopal Church. Six months later, the group reached close to fifteen thousand participants who regularly share news and notes about their congregations, videos and photos of community events, inspirational prayers and music, and other resources along with general encouragement to one another.

"I'm not a Pollyanna," Pogue says. "There has to be a place where we're working through difficulties. But the tone of that just became oppressive throughout the church, no matter where you stood on an issue. And it was amplified in the mass media where stories of controversy and dissent are more attention-grabbing."

An interim minister by vocation, Pogue comes easily to practices of defining identity in relation to the strengths of a community so that it can both affirm good work and feel adequately prepared to address challenges. Thus his approach to the negative tone he hears too often in discussions of the Episcopal Church draws from his experience with congregations in transition (and often crisis), where factions may have developed over time that are expressed more overtly in the search for new leadership for the church. "It helps to begin from an appreciative perspective," Pogue insists, "not to gloss over real problems, but to come at them from a place of strength and accomplishment. That's what I hoped to begin with the Facebook page."

To encourage this more positive ethos, Pogue posts a discussion question each week that invites people to reflect on their experiences as Episcopalians: "How does your church welcome people?" "What's your favorite passage from the Book of Common Prayer?" "What's your favorite hymn?" "What Episcopal churches have you attended on vacation?" "How do children participate in services at your church?" The questions are designed to invite sharing and collaboration, and to reinforce a participative practice of community enrichment across the church. But they start with a very particular "you"—people in the pews; people doing various kinds of lay and ordained ministry. "I'm very intentional in asking about *your* Episcopal Church," explains Pogue. "I don't ask for commentary on any particular issue. I want the page to be a place where people can tell their stories, ask questions of one another, and really draw out the best of what we're doing in the world."

In addition to weekly questions, Pogue posts passages from morning and evening prayer each day and shares videos of hymns and other liturgical elements. This, in turn, encourages conversation (and often prayer) among participants, and it has also invited them to shape the content of the page with their own visual materials and discussions. Perhaps more importantly, as is the case with the Facebook communities initiated by Russell and Yaw, digital participation on the "Unapologetically Episcopalian" page is not a substitute for local church participation. "People are speaking from their experience of the church in their community, and they're sharing that with others to enrich everyone's experience," says Pogue. "Their participation in the Facebook page helps to carry the prayer, fellowship, and celebration they have in their own churches through the week. It keeps it alive on a day-to-day basis." In essence, Pogue, like Yaw and Russell, is extending the social media ministry of

Paul by creating a digital epistolary space in which a much wider range of believers and seekers can include their own observations and experiences in an evolving, collective "Status Update from the Church in the Digital World."

Relational Communications 101:
Moving Toward Reformation Community

Across Facebook in particular, hundreds of mainline Christians are gathering in assorted affinity groups. Twenty-five hundred women gather in the "Presbyterian Women in the PC(USA)" group to share news, offer support, and narrate something of their own spiritual experience. Sixteen hundred "loyal radicals" in the Facebook page "Presbymergent" help each other to find congregations, understand change in the church, and feel more connected to both traditional and emergent practices of faith. More than twenty thousand Lutherans on the ECLA Facebook page swap perspectives on lived theology, social justice, and recipes for the perfect JELL-O salad. Close to a hundred thousand Methodists around the world visit the United Methodist Church Facebook page on a regular basis, and the United Church of Christ Facebook page hosts another fifty thousand.

The list could go on and on, but the point is that significantly more than two are gathered in these digital spaces, making up an important part of the Plural Who to whom religious leaders must attend and with whom they must engage. If you are somewhere in the formal leadership hierarchy of your church and you're not engaging these digital groups in some way, you're truly not attending to one of the most vital, active segments of your community. As Bishop Andy Doyle of the Episcopal Diocese of Texas insists, "I just don't think that churches will be successful in any way if they aren't successful in engaging this emerging part of our culture."

———

What format do you already engage: Facebook, Twitter, YouTube or another? How could you deepen that participation? Who might you and your community more actively engage in the Digital

Reformation? As you search through Facebook, Twitter, and You-Tube for keywords that are meaningful in your denomination or area of ministry, who stands out as potential new conversation partners? What do you hear and see when you actively attend to these new voices? What might you share as you more actively connect and engage with them?

In Part III we will delve further into how the shift from modern broadcast media practices to contemporary digital social media has had an impact on the nature of community in general and religious community in particular. From there, we will look at examples of how social media communications practices in the Digital Reformation allow for the enrichment and extension of communities of faith.

Part III

COMMUNITY IN THE DIGITAL REFORMATION

THE REFORMATION WILL
NOT BE TELEVISED

From Broadcast Consumption to Digital Connection

In the name of "progress," our official culture is striving to force the new media to do the work of the old.

—*Marshall McLuhan*

In Part II, we followed the evolution of media practices from premodern social reading to broadcast or mass media. That shift had plenty of impact on communications practices themselves. Of course, it also contributed to a progressive reshaping of social life that had significant consequences for modern notions of identity and community.

The subtleties of this process are what philosopher Marshall McLuhan had in mind in 1967 when he famously wrote, "the medium is the massage."[1] Though McLuhan wrote "the medium is the *message*" in an earlier publication, his later pun (which he attributed to a serendipitous printer's error) makes the point more clearly: The form of a medium in itself, independent of content, shifts our perception of reality and shapes our common habitus. The modern book—small, lightweight, inexpensive—made it easy for people to stroll off to read under a tree in a quiet meadow or linger over a story through the night by the candle's glow. At just a few pennies a pop, almost anyone could afford a book or two, or three, or four. Throw in a couple of incandescent light bulbs and indoor plumbing, and you're pretty much set for a solitary literary retreat.

In this way, the new medium changed not only the way we communicate. It changed the way we form—or neglect to form—community. The cultural shift facilitated by mechanized printing had a more direct spiritual impact, as well. In McLuhan's view, the rise of literacy as it was sponsored by the mass-produced book—the development of what he called "The Typographic Man"—associated rational thought with reading and decisively separated thinking from other human actions, or, we should probably say, from human *inter*actions. As a result, our very sense of the sacred abiding among us was gradually displaced into the shadowy landscape of the unreal. McLuhan maintained that in the process of private reading, the medium of the book was teaching us with its subtle *massage* that what was of value was that which we could see as separate from ourselves, delineate, and, ultimately, count. The act of "putting our thoughts on paper" or of "capturing an idea on the page" led us to believe that's where thoughts *really are*. Hence, thinking is *realized*—both achieved and made real—by writing down our thoughts and in reading the thoughts of others. To the extent that our spiritual experiences are often "beyond words," like many of the most significant qualities of our interpersonal relationships, they could not be claimed as phenomenon that functioned within the domain of modern rationality.

Both Romanticism in the eighteenth century and Transcendentalism in the nineteenth can be seen in this light as attempts by writers, artists, philosophers, and religionists to reconcile the cleavage set by the Enlightenment between imagination and reason, the sacred and the secular, or understanding and faith. When St. Anselm elaborated a philosophy of "faith seeking understanding" in the eleventh century, he didn't understand the two terms as opposites in a process that would give rational meaning to the sacred. Rather, he was describing a spiritual life in which "an active love of God seeking a deeper knowledge of God"[2] would be practiced.

By the twentieth century, the Romanian historian of religion Mircea Eliade had accepted a much sharper opposition between the sacred and the profane as the natural consequence of cultural progress that distinguished the religious nature of the inherently irrational "primitive man" from rational "modern man." Yet increasing inability to engage the sacred, and our romanticizing of "primitive" peoples with a keener "irrational" sense of the spiritual, McLuhan argued, had nothing to do with any inherent irrationality. They had everything to do with the way new media had taught us to devalue, and therefore to ignore, knowledge gained through sensory and relational experience, including religious or spiritual knowledge.[3]

Ultimately, a habitus centered on visually based, alphabetical thought accelerated by the printing press separated us not only from each other, but from our souls. As Robert Bellah explained in the 1970s, religion in the United States became a civic practice "much more related to order, law, and right than to salvation and love."[4] Unlike the believers who don't belong, or those who neither belong nor believe with any depth but who access lingering spiritual benefits vicariously through their use of religious symbols, Bellah saw "civic religion" in America after World War II as highlighting conformity with rules rather than any sort of spiritual practice of relational engagement. Through the 1960s and '70s, as broadcast media accelerated our disconnectedness, American civil religion itself waned considerably as the structuring force for public ethics.

Where It Turns Out Everybody Doesn't Actually Know Your Name: The Fantasy of Broadcast Community

There has always been a certain level of disconnectedness, at least on a functional level, between producers and consumers of communications media. All communication is mediated in some way. But the technologies that allowed the inexpensive, mass-produced book and, later, the increasingly smaller, more portable, and more affordable radio, television, music player, and so on have over time significantly separated us from each other in both real and metaphorical ways, so that we have come to forget the connective function of communications. The medieval mystic Julian of Norwich called this kind of coming together "one-ing." Although the word is often translated as "unifying" in Julian's *Showings*, its more common Middle English use was related to activities of gathering, as when a farmer took up the labor of "one-ing" sheaths of wheat into haystacks or a parent "oned" the children home to supper. God the Father, God the Son, and God the Holy Spirit were "oned" in the Trinity as an active verb rather than "one" as a fixed noun.[5]

Yet the effect of mass communications generally and broadcast communications in particular has been to diminish the role of interactive engagement—of community—in day-to-day communication. Even when two or three people are watching TV together in the same room, they are not necessarily sharing an experience. In place of the sorts of interpersonal, communal engagements that premodern people had with books, music, theater, and the like—as we saw in Chapter 3—we loosely aligned ourselves to various "stars" whose charismatic personalities and endorsed products have stood in for the one-to-one-to-two-to-one-to-three-to-one-to-two-to-one constellations of families, friends, churches, and communities that once characterized our lives together.

Take, for instance, the friendly neighborhood pub in the popular 1980s sitcom *Cheers*, where Sam Malone nursed the tap for a gathering of regulars. Well before widespread internet communities developed, Sam's bar functioned as a televised virtual meeting place that allowed disconnected Americans to imagine themselves into community. But the virtual nature of this experience is twice-removed: Viewers imagined themselves into a community that, first, was fictional and, second, that could have no awareness of the reality of any particular viewer. The fantasy of the neighborhood pub community was further detached from lived reality when it was absorbed into the popular animated sitcom *The Simpsons* in the 1990s as "Moe's Tavern," a place "Where nobody knows your name." Unlike the characters in *Cheers*, those at Moe's are not portrayed by real people, yet we come to think of them as "friends" as well, and we can often describe their various qualities and quirks more easily than we can those of close family members.

Indeed, evolutionary psychologist Satoshi Kanazawa argues that "the human brain has difficulty distinguishing real friends and

people they see on TV." Our engagement with television characters and other celebrities is not necessarily shallow. It's not real,
of course, but our brains have not (yet) evolved to tell the difference between a real friend and a television "friend." This has to do
not only with the frequency with which we may watch television
(or movies), but with the visual, aural, emotional, and social presentation of television characters. In evolutionary terms, the cues
sent by our favorite "Desperate Housewife" are not any different
from those sent by Sally-from-the-block—other than that they're
more interesting. Hence our urgency to ditch our flesh-and-blood
friends or the Thursday soup social at church so we can get home
to check in on the beleaguered castaways on *Lost*. Says Kanazawa,
"Watching TV is our form of participating in civic groups because
we do not really know that we are not participating in them." By
extension, people who engage religion primarily through broadcast media don't necessarily see themselves as "not belonging" to
a church.[6]

Mass Is Now Over: Why Small Is the New Big

Despite concerns that social media platforms like Facebook
and Twitter distort concepts of friendship, it turns out that such
engagements invite a real intimacy that stands in stark contrast to
the fantasy friendships encouraged by broadcast media. Cameron
Marlow, an in-house sociologist who studies user behavior on
Facebook, has found that, though the average Facebook user has
about 120 "friends," she or he interacts regularly with only seven
to ten of them. Even users with 500 "friends" or more limit regular
interaction to 5 to 10 percent of them.[7]

Indeed, evolutionary anthropologist Robin Dunbar has developed a model to show the optimal number of people with whom
we can have relationships "involving trust and obligation [in
which] there's some personal history, not just names and places."[8]
The so-called "Dunbar Number" that emerges from the model,
which correlates primate brain size to community size, is 150.
Even within that number, intense relationships of intimacy are relatively few—5 to 10 percent, it turns out. Meaningful, maintainable

friendships and other relationships of the more casual sort top out at somewhere between forty and sixty people. A number of new social networking sites have in fact taken the Dunbar Number to heart in challenges to Facebook and Twitter that focus on providing social media that enhance communications and relationships among smaller cohorts of closer friends, family members, and colleagues.[9]

Once we get beyond 150 contacts, institutional structures become necessary to ensure civility and safety. You need an official monitor for your Facebook page to weed out spammers, flamers, or bullies. You post announcements or send out broadcast emails to all of the members, hoping they all won't respond. Not long ago, a friend with some fifteen hundred followers on Twitter—hardly a number that would put her at the top of the Twitterati heap—complained that she was being inundated with replies and direct messages from followers. "Even if I only tweet every couple hours, and only ten people reply to each tweet, I have dozens and dozens of messages to deal with during the day—messages from people I don't really even know."

The truth is that the more friends or group page members one has on Facebook, or the more followers one has on Twitter, the more likely communications with those contacts are to have the anonymous, one-to-many tone of broadcast relationships. Because we've tended to map our experience with broadcast media onto the digital domain, we tend to see the power of new social media sites as lying in an ability to connect us with more and more and more people. That capability is certainly there, and we have seen again and again that it is able to have remarkable effects in relatively short-term events. The gathering of millions around the world in prayers of hope and thanksgiving for thirty-three men rescued from a Chilean mine in the fall of 2010, or the initial digital donations from people around the world in response to the earthquake that ravaged much of Haiti earlier in the year, are but two of many examples. Digital media have allowed people to do more than report on events. They are able to actively shape them on social media sites that cross the barriers of traditional media by connecting ordinary people who participate digitally as events unfold.

But what is most remarkable about digital social media is how they allow us to maximize smallness in number and what would traditionally have been seen as a significant lack of power and leadership. One of the great gifts of these new technologies is their ability to bring together people who in the broadcast age would not have had the critical mass, deep pockets, and technical wherewithal required to gain access to the kinds of resources that now allow small clusters of people to tell their story, connect across geographic distance, and reinforce the bonds of affiliation and affection that ground community. The smallness of the average mainline church allows it to engage in modes of communication that deepen members' knowledge of and connection to one another and the church they embody. This can happen in both face-to-face and digital environments.

Mainline Christianity Behind Closed Doors: From Modern Invisibility to Digital Transparency

Technology anthropologist Stefana Broadbent argues that social media breaks through "an imposed isolation" created by the geographically distributed reality of institutional settings as they developed after the Industrial Revolution.[10] We come to think that we are only "at church" when we are physically at the church building. We see the church buildings as indicators of a distinctiveness that amounts to separateness for late modern people used to retreating to the privacy of the homes as distinguished from the public settings of their work or study. I go to this church. You go to that one, over there. And those people way out wherever they are? I have no idea where they go to church.

In effect, the segregation of churches into designated built spaces has made active and engaged religious or spiritual practice somewhat invisible in the wider world—an invisibility that religious historian Cynthia M. Baker argues is internalized by those who occupy or use these buildings.[11] The stark evidence of this internalized invisibility for many mainline Christians is the wrenching discomfort when an Evangelical companion insists on praying before lunch *in public*. The awkwardness we may feel at such moments is part of a culturally negotiated mainline habitus that allows that, while we might be Christians all the time, we only present ourselves as such behind closed church doors.

Digital social media practices that highlight more extensive personal and institutional transparency can thus cause us to feel exposed and vulnerable when they bring together parts of our lives that have long been rendered separate by the modern affection for distinction and isolation of what, as the Enlightenment and the Industrial Revolution rolled on into the Atomic Age, were increasingly seen as inherently separate spheres of life. As Broadbent notes, this aided in commercial productivity because workers were no longer at risk of distraction from fussy children, nosey neighbors, or the clanging of the local church bell for prayer through the hours of the day. This idea of separation becomes more durably normalized as activities that do not clearly contribute to civic or commercial life are hidden away from view as "private" activities not meant to be discussed in polite society. For mainline Protestants, who have garnered the greatest cultural, social, and economic benefit from the effects of modern secularization and associated separation, it is understandable that new modes of communication that foster more open, engaged community would be particularly uncomfortable.

Acts of Media Uniformity:
How Broadcast Communication Practices Promote Sameness

Now, of course all of this doesn't track neatly back to the printing press, from which mountains of good have certainly come. But it is clearly the case that, as much as the mass communication era contributed to the rise of literacy, religious freedom, democracy, and all sorts of social goods, it also contributed significantly to a dramatic reconfiguring of relationships and communities by changing a fundamental element of human communication. To extend McLuhan's claim that "the medium is the massage/message," the message massages the mind so that how we see and respond to ourselves, each other, and the world—our basic human consciousness—changes, as well. The historian and philosopher Walter Ong insisted in his classic exploration of the shift from oral to written culture, *Orality and Literacy*, "More than any other single invention, writing has transformed human consciousness."[12] While it may or may not be the case that the most transformative invention in terms of human awareness of self and other has been writing—the jury is still out on cultural, neurological, and other effects of digital media—it is clear that human sentience is uniquely tied to communication practices, so that any dramatic change in the dominant mode of communication will impact human consciousness of self and other.

Ong argued that radio and television had ushered in a "secondary orality" that harkened back to the relational sense of preliterate cultures, while at the same time maintaining a close relationship to the characteristics of print culture that made people more anonymous to one another. In Ong's view, modern mass media was able to "foster . . . a communal *sense*" that, while not requiring actual engagement with others, did encourage a certain depth of sensitivity to others. Pursuing a line of thinking that is reinforced in Kanazawa's more recent research, Ong observed that, though the audience for radio and television is "absent, invisible, inaudible," presenters "accommodate themselves to the psychology of the media,"[13] which insists that no one seem especially different or controversial. In turn, audience members adapt their own behavior in a more socially conforming direction.

The connection we feel to media personalities, false though it may be, weirdly replicates certain characteristics of the medieval *habitus* of obedience. Instead of the thwap-thwap-thwap of Master Elwin's birch rods, however, identification with celebrities reinforced by what we all know as "peer pressure" keeps us more or less in line—especially in line at the mall, where we're able to buy all the things media personalities have assured us we need to "fit in." Exploration, innovation, and the other good stuff that characterized much of the Enlightenment have over time largely been awarded to various sorts of élites—actors, athletes, entertainers, writers, and a narrow band of scholars—while most of the rest of us merely get to watch from behind the televised sidelines. They don't call it "programming" for nothing.[14]

Our attraction to virtual "friendships" with media personalities is illustrated nowhere more clearly than in the explosion of

reality television shows that have dominated the broadcast market over the past decade or so. My own hunch is that, as people
have become more and more involved in creating their own digital
media presences that challenge the celebrity of commercial media,
reality shows have allowed broadcasters to amp up the attachments Ong and Kanazawa describe by presenting more and more
"celebrities" who seem "just like us." Over time, it seems, we've
come to understand that our lives are probably not so much
like those of the coffeehouse trendies of *Friends* or the medical
miracle workers of *Grey's Anatomy*, but maybe we're not so different from whomever our most recent favorite is on *Survivor* or
The Bachelor. The goal seems to be to progressively move the
line between reality and fantasy so that we come to see our whole
lives as having meaning only to the extent that they connect to the
"reality" presented on broadcast programs. Evangelical Christian
broadcasters have picked up on this trend by entering the reality
television genre with the popular program *The Way of the Master*,
on which former teen heartthrob Kirk Cameron and atheist-slayer
Ray Comfort take to the streets to teach "real-life witnessing in
action" to ordinary believers.

Despite constant protests about the depravity of contemporary broadcast media, the disconnectedness facilitated by virtual
attachment to on-screen personalities is ideal for churches and
religious leaders whose theologies highlight conformity with
narrowly defined moral codes and life practices. Pat Robertson,
Mother Angelica, or other celebrities of religious media might rant
about sex, foul language, violence (when they're not using their
own incendiary language to describe or encourage various sorts of
"spiritual warfare"), and other objectionable content in popular
media. But they are nonetheless beneficiaries of a mass media consciousness developed out of passive, top-down-driven consumption
of images and ideologies from celebrities whom media consumers
could think of as "friends."

This model of media has actively encouraged conformity, dis-
couraged critical reflection, and, until the advent of digital media,
made real interaction with religious personalities or others in their
audience nearly impossible. The mass media model was thus,

until very recently, the perfect vehicle for shaping the theological and social viewpoints of millions and millions of people in North America and, increasingly, around the world, who would provide ongoing financial support for broadcast ministries. It is remarkably effective for religious leaders who tend to "view the world from a relatively narrow frame of moral reference" that encourages both producers and consumers of Evangelical Christian media to "shun self-criticism while hurling insults at nonconformists even within their own ranks," according to Quentin J. Schultze and Robert H. Woods, Jr., who study Evangelical media practices.[15] What's more, the beauty of vicarious participation in a faith community—even one professing relatively restrictive behavioral norms—is that neither fellow devotees nor revered religious leaders are in a position to evaluate an individual's actual practice of faith in the context of real relationships and communities, whether these are enacted in face-to-face or digital environments.

Leading Beyond the Boundaries:
Reviving Community with Social Communication

Digital social media has changed all that. Dramatically. Digital social media is a very different kind of communication innovation with very different community implications. Indeed, it's different even than the internet as we understood it through the development of email in the 1980s and of online searching in the 1990s. The early models of internet-based communication assumed that digital technology merely allowed the mechanisms of broadcast media to happen more rapidly, more globally, and in a constant, overlapping stream of interruption.

While it's taken us a while to begin to learn this, digital social media are not in fact just the next step on the continuum of mass communication technologies that moved in relatively short order from the printing press to the radio to the television. Digital technology as it is used in the context of social media sites like Facebook, Twitter, YouTube, Flickr, and in the text messaging features and applications on smartphones, are back-to-the-future affairs that have profoundly interrupted the progressive disconnectedness of social life that has characterized modernity since the ascendency of the printing press. Like medieval manuscripts, these new media are at their roots social. They are designed—or, more accurately, have emerged with the ability—to facilitate connectedness, sharing, collaboration, and the construction of new modes of community that transcend traditional geographic, national, linguistic, class, gender, and a whole host of other physical and social boundaries that print and broadcast media tended to reinforce. It is in this way that many of the comparisons between social media and the printing press largely get it wrong.

When we think of new digital social media as being like the printing press, or when early online innovators thought of the internet as TV on steroids, we and they were, as McLuhan saw in the 1960s, "striving to force the new media to do the work of the old."[16] Thus, churches that see websites or Facebook group pages as replacements for Yellow Pages listings, or imagine sermon blogs as a way of connecting potential members to the physical church and its community, fail to harness the tremendous power of new digital social media platforms that function on the basis of distributed participation rather than passive consumption. Such efforts encourage socially disengaged seekers and believers to participate vicariously in the church community without really inviting them to bring their own perspectives, ideas, talents, and other gifts into a creative process of practicing church together in communities that span physical and digital domains.

———

This raises a number of important questions for Christians today who hope to make the most of new modes of media and associated communication practices to enrich and extend community. To what extent, for instance, are the stories we share in our communities focused on connecting to particular personalities—Jesus, the apostles or saints, a bishop or spiritual celebrity—rather than the social and spiritual practices that make these individuals compelling? To what extent have we come to understand "growth" as a predominantly numerical phenomenon that invites us to mute the distinctiveness of people as we slot them into manageable demographic clusters? How can we combine the virtue of smallness with practices of digital communication that reinforce more intimate interpersonal connections within and across communities? How might we extend our spiritual practice in both local and digital spaces so that our churches, as expressions of committed Christian practice, can avoid the social and cultural invisibility and isolation that have increasingly rendered us irrelevant in everyday life?

In the next chapter, we will explore further the implications of new digital social media practices for facilitating the development, enrichment, and extension of community across boundaries that thrive in our lingering, late modern broadcast habitus.

6

DIOS NO TIENE FRONTERAS[*]

Practicing Community in the Digital Reformation

> God never told the world to go to church; but God did tell the church
> to go to the world.
>
> *—Sharon Watkins*

On Labor Day in Sedona, shards of cloud tossed easy shadows over the red rocks and saltbush along the banks of Oak Creek. I know this not because I spent the weekend hiking along the canyon trails, but because Kirk Smith, the Bishop of the Episcopal Diocese of Arizona, did. In the photos he posted on Facebook, the hills glowed with a tranquility that would take somewhat more effort to call up in heated, late summer Arizona days ahead.

Earlier in the year, the governor of Arizona had signed a controversial law that requires local and state law enforcement officers to question people about their immigration status if the officers believe there is reason to suspect someone of being in the country without legal visitor or immigrant status. The law also makes it a state crime to be in the United States illegally. Well before the bill was signed into law, religious leaders spoke against it, among them Smith, who has insisted that immigration is "the civil rights issue of our time."

---

* "God Has No Borders"

Trinity Cathedral in Phoenix was an epicenter of religious action in the days before the bill's passage and in the aftermath. And in the late summer, Smith would travel with the presiding bishop of the Episcopal Church, Katharine Jefferts Schori, and twenty-seven other bishops, their partners, and spouses to the Arizona-Mexico border for a three-day immersion trip that would reveal something of the reality of life and the challenges of ministry for people living on the hardscrabble geography. Throughout the pilgrimage and in the days after, as the House of Bishops of the Episcopal Church gathered for an annual meeting in Phoenix, Smith posted hastily edited videos, photos, and brief notes about the engagement between the bishops and the borderland communities on his Facebook page.

In Smith's Facebook community, his participation in the immersion trip had a powerful resonance. Each time he posted, friends shared prayers for the bishops and for the migrants they hoped to serve with their witness. Indeed, the counter-intuitive reality is that outside of social media platforms like Facebook and Twitter, it would be impossible for Smith and other leaders in ministry to so richly witness to the significance of face-to-face relationship and spiritual presence across the diverse communities that come together as the Church in the world.

The digital engagement of Smith's Facebook community also had meaning for members of borderland congregations and ministries that have been providing assistance to immigrants for many years, often without much notice from the rest of the church. Said one minister from a border community: "We're all like ghosts out here in the desert, floating around invisibly. Maybe that's why we're so frightening to so many people. But when people come to see us here, they see not just ghosts, but embodied spirits. Living beings. People on the same earth with them. The issues we face are just ideas, political concerns, unless other people see that we actually exist as human beings."

In a very small and preliminary way, the photos, videos, and short comments posted by Smith and others who participated in the immersion trip broadened and enriched the church as community, because it shared something of the embodied, located reality of borderland existence. Smith's digital witness functions as a conduit for deeper relationship among people who *already have meaningful affinities*—affinities they may not notice beyond their local church communities or outside of the Sunday service. Smith's witness moves his digital ministry from listening and attending to more actively connecting and engaging across online and offline geographies. In this case, he offers a spiritual and ethical engagement that brings together digital and multiple face-to-face communities that would not otherwise cross paths. In this way, Smith's digital witness breaks through the effects of modern spiritual isolation and invisibility described in the previous chapter.

For the most part, the friends on the bishop's Facebook page, his Twitter feed, and those who subscribe to his monthly "e-pistle" blog (which is emailed to a thousand or so subscribers and made available on the diocesan website) have connected with him in the digital domain because they have an existing ecclesial relationship with him. They may not be close personal friends, but they know him in a very particular context and they share at least a substantially common commitment to Christian practice.

Smith's witness strengthens his own ties to these people as a leader in the diocese and in the wider church, but it also contributes to the development of their relationship to each other across the diocesan and church community. The witness he shares is meaningful because it happens in the context of real relationships that extend to other real relationships. Because his Facebook page, Twitter feed, and blog have made Smith more known and knowable to those in his diocese, across the Episcopal Church, and in wider interreligious contexts, he creates an intimate rather than a popular mass appeal. What centuries of political influence that reached a zenith early in the broadcast era have massaged us into forgetting is that Christianity is not meant to be a popular religion. It's meant to be an intimate one—so intimate, in fact, with those on the margins of society that it is bound to fail at communications, community, and leadership practices that aim to build popularity.

Translating Reformation

Our deeply traditional claim to practices of relational intimacy is at the center of any hope we might have of developing ministries that effectively integrate digital and face-to-face engagement. In fact, fostering relational intimacy is significantly more important in socially networked communications than in mass communications, because ideas in the social media world are passed on from friend to friend on the basis of the relevance of the idea in those particular relationships. I share a post, photo, news story, or other material on my Facebook page or Twitter feed because I think it will matter to the cohort I have developed in these settings. And, because it matters to my friends, I will probably have something to say about it, and so will many of my friends. The content I share, that is, contributes to our relationship, whether that relationship is enacted primarily online, offline, or across both domains.

When a formal representative of the Church posts images from borderland ministries on Facebook, he enlarges the Church as community, bridging quite separate spheres of life, ministry, and meaning within and across geographically, culturally, and even temporally separated communities. Another subtle community practice is going on in Smith's digital witness, as well. When he posts about the struggle of undocumented immigrants and those who minister to them, Smith is in effect giving over his episcopal authority to them. He is ceding institutional space to those on the furthest margins of that space. "The first problem of the media is posed by what does not get translated, or even published in the dominant political languages,"[1] the philosopher Jacques Derrida taught. Nor the dominant spiritual and religious languages, we might note.

This, of course, was very much at the center of the sixteenth-century Reformations, focused as they were on ensuring that scripture was available to every believer and seeker in a language she or he could understand. But in broader structural terms, the Reformations tended to reinforce distinction in geography, ethnicity, class, and other social factors to an extent that is still abundantly clear throughout most of our churches today. Hence the enduring relevance of the old truism, "eleven o'clock on Sunday morning is the most segregated hour of the week."[2]

By witnessing to life on the border, Smith reverses the direction of this reformational translation by opening what are certainly now *the* dominant media spaces to voices that would not readily be heard as specifically spiritual and religious voices. Bibles in their native languages people on the border have aplenty. What they don't have enough of are people who can translate their stories, with words and images, for believers from dominant demographics who can only follow the call to stand with those on the margins if they can hear their voices and see their faces. Smith thus uses the hierarchy to act on the witness in which he has participated and which he presents to an even wider community of witnesses. If, as Augustine reminded us, "God is a circle whose center is everywhere and whose circumference is nowhere,"[3] we can only assume that God's church is meant to be similarly organized—hierarchies not withstanding.

Digital Prophets: The Ethics of Extended Community

Enriching the spiritual lives of those within our established circles is not the only—nor, indeed, the primary—purpose of Christian community. After all, we are called to be "friends of God, *and prophets*" (Wisdom 7:27). In Smith's digital witness we see the importance of new social media for enacting this prophetic call.

As it happens, the borderland pilgrimage got little coverage outside of Arizona or Episcopal Church news outlets, and Smith was too engaged in the immersion itself to offer much by way of textual narration on his Facebook page or Twitter feed. Nevertheless, the images he shared of local community members, clergy, and others who minister to the hundreds of children, women, and men who attempt the dangerous migration into the United States each year were powerful reminders for his Facebook friends of the moral commitments he makes on behalf of his diocese and in the service of the wider Church.

Such images, and the words that may accompany them, do more than illustrate a social or political stance. They communicate core social justice values. Beyond this, when Smith shares words or images related to his ministry in the wider world—perhaps especially when this ministry is related to a complex and controversial issue like immigration reform—he models a kind of moral and spiritual transparency that itself expresses an important communication value that strengthens community. In this way, his practice is an act of witness that crosses multiple boundaries: between the merely social to the deeply ethical; between those who see issues differently in his local and extended communities; and, importantly, between distributed digital engagement and local face-to-face practice.

Witnessing Activism versus Acting on Witness

Now, to be clear, I am not equating the witness Kirk Smith offered through his Facebook page and Twitter feed to activism proper. As far as I know, no one hopped out from behind her desk or gave up his table at the local coffeehouse to trek to the Arizona border on the basis of Smith's updates. Near as I can tell, donations did not start pouring into the various churches and agencies doing the hard day-in-day-out work of providing food, shelter, legal support, medical care, and other necessities in borderland communities (though participating bishops did marshal resources from their own dioceses for those living and ministering on the border). Indeed, critics have increasingly complained that "social media activism" is fraught with the same problems as vicarious religious practice: It lets people have the feeling of involvement without requiring them to actually be involved.

In a 2010 *New Yorker* article, Malcolm Gladwell complained that social media activism is ineffective because, first, social networks rely on weak interpersonal ties among people who have only negligible commitment to a particular issue or community.[4] So, for instance, I can "like" the "Free Tibet" group or join the "1 Million Strong AGAINST the Arizona Immigration Law" group on Facebook without having to actually *do* anything to address the issues represented by these groups. I don't have to give money or march or provide food. Indeed, I don't even have to go as far as to comment on the group pages. Largely, this is because my connection to the other people supporting the cause is weak—I don't really know them outside of the social media setting and don't, therefore, feel a sense of obligation to these people to act upon the commitment I have professed by joining a Facebook group. It's not as though I'm likely to run into any of them at church on Sunday.

Second, Gladwell argues that social media activism is ineffective because the nature of networked communication is inherently anti-hierarchical. This, he maintains, limits effective organization, decision-making, problem-solving, and other critical elements of a movement for social transformation. He insists that "if you're taking on a powerful and organized establishment you have to be a hierarchy." I'm reasonably sure that Gladwell is confusing hierarchy with any form of structure and organization that supports collective problem-solving, decision-making, and action. Difficult though it is to sustain, the Quaker model of consensus-based decision-making has long testified to alternatives to hierarchical practice. In any case, Gladwell's point is that the loose structure of social media communities makes it difficult to understand who does exactly what, who has authority to start or stop any particular action, and who might have the final say on how the community as a whole expresses itself in words, images, and actions.

In many ways, Gladwell and other critics of social media activism are right. Social media practices are unlikely, on their own, to develop the strong personal ties and shared personal commitments that are essential to sustained, meaningful social transformation. On their own, they do not allow for the development of functional structures that facilitate action across digital and physical landscapes that are necessary for durable change. Indeed, most of the amazing examples we have seen of mass social media action that have effected change have been based on weak ties and minimal active commitment.

The backers of Barack Obama, for instance, were able to play a meaningful role in the presidential campaign by contributing only a few dollars each, or by heightening awareness by simply posting campaign updates on their Facebook pages and Twitter feeds.

Beyond this, their contributions amounted mainly to giving the campaign access to their online networks for further fundraising appeals. Though it certainly happened that many new relationships were formed among Obama supporters, the goal of the campaign's use of social media was not to build among supporters a sustained commitment to each other, or even to the issues that motivated them to participate, but to the candidate as a candidate. There was a campaign hierarchy making decisions about what messages to highlight, what images to share, when to prompt followers to share, and so on. But they had no direct control over how supporters would represent the campaign within their own networks, and that really didn't matter much.

Overall, as the online encyclopedia Wikipedia testifies, the relatively small efforts of a very large number of people aggregate in support of a very small number of people who provide the larger commitment necessary to make things happen. This is actually the beauty of the new digital reality for those who see it in the most positive light. Critics, however, see it as part of an increasing erosion of interpersonal intimacy and real social engagement.

So, does Kirk Smith's posting on his borderland immersion pilgrimage contribute more to a false engagement with social justice issues or to a real commitment and involvement in transformation? Arguably, I'm biased here. I think that Smith organized and communicated important work that extends well beyond the political issues that swirled around the trip to the border to engage, enrich, and extend community. That said, I would suggest that the starting point for Smith's digital community—established communities with as many meaningful spiritual, historical, and theological affinities as they have cultural, political, and economic differences—is an important component in the effectiveness of his witness. It allows that his digital practice moves beyond the mere witness of activism to an act of witness that genuinely strengthens the Church as a community of justice and hope. Translating this witness into action by others across his diocese and in the wider Church is clearly a challenge, but this digital beginning creates a valuable platform for continuing dialogue and participation.

Practicing the Borderless Church

While Smith's practice of digital witness from the U.S./Mexico border was not part of a tightly choreographed social media engagement strategy, several principles emerge from his loosely integrated use of Facebook, Twitter, blogging, and the diocesan website:

- **Start where you are.** Smith shared news of the border immersion pilgrimage with natural communities of interest that connected to other communities of interest.
- **Be exactly who you are.** Schmaltzy though this sounds, it's critical. The truth is that, based on his Facebook posts, I'd never hire Kirk Smith to write marketing copy, create videos, or take photos. And that's pretty much exactly why his Facebook page is compelling. He's trying to be a better minister in his community, not a better marketer to it.
- **Build bridges.** Smith used his Facebook page and blog to connect people in his diocese to ministries that are geographically and often spiritually on the margins of the church and to give those ministries a voice in the wider church. This practice connected not only the "center" to the "margins," but revealed the connectedness of the separate communities that make up the center itself.
- **Show more than you tell.** Images, more than words alone, evoke emotions and engage others. They don't have to be brilliant works of cinematography or photojournalism. If videos are under two minutes and if photos have captions, you're in pretty good shape.
- **Practice the ministry you profess.** A key goal of the border immersion experience was to connect the wider church to the often isolated border communities. Smith extended this experience by sharing videos of the pilgrimage that enabled people on the border to tell their stories in their own words.

Seeing & Believing: Imaging the Digital Reformation

In much smaller, less dramatic ways, Smith enacts this informal strategy frequently on his Facebook page with notes about and photos of the changing skies and seasonal landscapes of the Arizona desert. "Heavy thunderstorms in Sedona right now," he might post from the road, along with a photo of a red and purple sky above the mountains. His Facebook photo galleries are testimonies to his grounded, embodied practice with real people in his diocese and well beyond. Here he is walking on an Oregon beach during a vacation. Here we see the view from his hotel room in Minneapolis, there with his wife at a picnic with kids from the diocese.

It's not all travelogue, however. Album after album of photos on Smith's Facebook page show the people he encounters in his life as a bishop—dozens and dozens and dozens of them, like so many saints named in Paul's letters. Most of the photos are not actually posted by Smith himself, but by those he meets in his travels. The photos witness, then, to a convergent practice of listening, attending, connecting, and engaging across digital and physical boundaries.

In their own ways, these photos are not unlike the "cup holders of the Digital Reformation" we discussed in Chapter 1—small innovations in day-to-day practice that are gradually changing how we live our lives and practice our faith together (in this case, without all the fast-food calories). People practice an interactive, co-creative habitus throughout the wider context of their lives, regardless of whether they happen to be communicating, connecting, and collaborating within a digital sphere or a face-to-face one.

For Smith, whose congregations are spread across notoriously rugged physical and cultural terrain, social media allow an attention to relationships that would otherwise be difficult to offer on a number of levels. He stays in close touch, for example, with a group of Navajo teens in a remote area of the diocese. "They're the future leaders of the church," he says. "They have a commitment to their community, and their heritage, and the church unlike anything I've seen. We have to be there for them. We have to be accessible." Through Facebook, Smith is able to check goings-on in the community, answer questions, point out resources, and otherwise be in an ongoing conversation that sustains a vital relationship. And, of course, as Smith enacts this relationship in digital space, those in his digital community are privy to much of it, this, too, serving as a kind of witness to and bridging of the church as diverse and unified Body of Christ.

Here again, the relational advantage of smallness reveals itself. I looked recently at the Facebook page of a writer who has close to twenty thousand "friends." She has another forty-five thousand Twitter followers, about three hundred of whom she follows. Realistically, how much can she possibly be aware of what's going on in the lives of what are surely social media crowds, but hardly communities? Such a haul of friends and followers makes Smith's digital media posse seem more than paltry. But the truth is that it allows him to be in contact in meaningful ways that go well beyond setting TweetDeck to send an automated message crafted by your communications director to all your friends and followers with a new insight or inspiration every four hours.

———

In Kirk Smith's digital witness on the U.S./Mexico border we see one of the content overlaps that I warned about in the Introduction. As a formally designated leader in the church, Smith used new digital communication practices to enrich and extend community. There's really no telling exactly where leadership practice starts and communication or community practice begins. In the next section, we focus more specifically on denominational distinctions that have defined characteristic approaches to leadership in mainline churches. In Chapter 7, then, we consider how the Reformation roots of mainline churches shape leadership that is highly adaptable to digital settings before exploring, in Chapter 8, examples of leaders today whose digital ministries echo the practices of those in the early Church who themselves attempted to minister in the context of dramatic cultural change.

Before moving on, however, take a moment to consider these questions: What impact would most people in your faith community say social media have on their intimate relationships? How is social media linking you to wider and wider communities, or reinforcing bonds within your community? Moving deeper, you might ask what groups or clusters of individuals are on the margins of your community? How might you attend to them and connect more deeply by using new social media practices? How can you bring these voices into your local community, both in its face-to-face manifestation and in its digital locales? How might this change your community—enrich and extend it?

Part IV

LEADERSHIP FOR THE
DIGITAL REFORMATION

TOWARD THE TWEETHOOD
OF ALL BELIEVERS

The Past & Future Reformation of
Mainline Leadership Practice

History cannot give us a program for the future, but it can give us a fuller understanding of ourselves, and of our common humanity, so that we can better face the future.

—Robert Penn Warren

October 13, 2010 turns out to have been a remarkable day in postmodern history—one of those days that many of us will remember for a very long time. Some will call it a miraculous day, the day thirty-three men who had been trapped in a Chilean mine for sixty-nine days were hoisted safely to the earth's surface while millions and millions of people watched live streaming video of the rescue on computers, laptops, and smartphones around the world. Web traffic monitoring services reported some four million page views per minute during the final hours of the rescue—topping online viewership for the funeral of pop star Michael Jackson and coming close to the pace of online activity during the inauguration of Barack Obama.

Throughout a rescue that extended across the world clock, people did more than watch passively, absorbing the images from the mine and the commentary from television personalities (though the rescue was certainly a broadcast bonanza, too). Rather, in the digital world, millions of people following the miners' rescue in "Fénix 2," the high-tech sarcophagus in which they ascended like so many Lazaruses from the tomb of a mine some two thousand feet below the earth's surface, also prayed. More particularly, they prayed together.

On the Facebook group page "Chilean Miners," developed by an Austrian online marketing consultant, more than sixty-five hundred people participated in prayer and conversation throughout the day of the rescue, and continued to connect in the weeks after. Unlike many other Facebook group pages, where people often post without engaging others in the group beyond a periodic click of the "like" thumbs-up, members of the "Chilean Miners" page were remarkably interactive, with nearly every post receiving multiple comments from other participants across the globe.

All this spiritual and social digital dialogue around the Chilean miners' rescue made clear that, as we all were engaging the remarkable ascent of the miners from darkness, we were also participating in the ascent of digital social media over broadcast media. What's more, to the extent that the global narrative developing throughout and beyond the rescue was significantly spiritual in nature, we were witnessing what was arguably the most significant global spiritual conversation that had ever taken place on earth. This was not religious television. It was a massive expression of a new digital spiritual reality.

A Reformation Without Leaders?:
Why Leadership Today Requires Basic Digital Literacy

What was striking to me, as I observed this digital spiritual emergence, was how few religious leaders participated in the prayers and conversations about the rescue through the day. I scanned the pages of my own Facebook friends, a large percentage of whom are pastors, priests, bishops, lay leaders, religion scholars, seminary

professors, and God geeks more generally. One leader, who generally offers robust religious insight and invites regular engagement
through her Twitter feed and Facebook page, was in the midst of
an extended conversation about what "mission" means today. She
never looked up. Another touted camps and conference centers
in his denomination. Another still was prepping for an upcoming church conference. An urban minister tracked a long day of
travel across a world that was mostly focused on the miners' rescue. Two separate religion writers discussed their new books about
the emerging church, apparently unaware of the spiritual practice
emerging around them. An editor added to her cache of friends, as
did a seminary professor. A pastor fretted over weekend sermon
prep and asked for advice from friends.

On and on went the unscientific survey of my five hundred or
so, mostly mainline, churchy friends. In the end, only two took digital notice of the rescue and its spiritual significance. One, a seminary
professor, reposted the quote on the backs of the miners' t-shirts
from Psalm 95—*En su mano están las profundidades de la tierra;
suyas son las alturas de los montes.* ("In his hand are the depths
of the earth; the heights of the mountains are also his.") Another,
a priest with a long record of social activism, celebrated the thirty-
third miner's release from the rescue capsule. Both shared their brief
commentary on their own Facebook walls rather than in the digital
gathering places that had arisen all across the web. And, of course,
there I was, observing it all, noting the release of each miner, com-
menting on my Facebook page, but not otherwise engaging.

After a full day of joy not only in the rescue of the miners, but
also in the eagerness of people around the world to enact the very
best qualities of the Digital Reformation to gather, converse, pray,
and develop relationships that nurture and sustain their faith, my
observation of the church's lack of leadership or even participation
in the spiritual reality playing out across digital space was a bit of
a comedown. I couldn't help but recall a somewhat similar digital
leadership lapse earlier in the year, when Pope Benedict XVI issued
a message to the Roman Catholic faithful in which he encouraged
priests to proclaim the Gospel by employing the latest generation
of audio-visual resources by way of opening broad new vistas for

dialogue, evangelization, and catechesis. The pope's message for the forty-fourth World Communications Day highlighted the centrality of the priest in engaging new social media in the service of the Church[1]

"Who better than a priest, as a man of God, can develop and put into practice, by his competence in current digital technology, a pastoral outreach capable of making God concretely present in today's world and presenting the religious wisdom of the past as a treasure which can inspire our efforts to live in the present with dignity while building a better future?" the pope had asked in his message to the faithful.

Meanwhile, back in the digital Vatican, "P2Y" (Pope to You), a website created by the Pontifical Council for Social Communications that is directed to young people, seemed to have inadvertently inverted the hierarchy the pope sought to reinforce. With embedded glitzy, multiplatform technologies from YouTube videos to an iPhone application, P2Y encouraged Roman Catholic teens and young adults to post the pope's message on their Facebook pages and to send it to their priest via email. The site also provided versions that kids could print out and take or "snail mail"—deliver via local post—to priests who remain hopelessly unplugged from the wired world.

Who Better?:
Distributed Authority & Leadership in the Digital Reformation

The answer to the pope's "who better?" question was apparently this: a fifteen-year-old with a laptop, a Facebook account, and a Wi-Fi connection.

In effect, the P2Y site gives lie to the reality of digital practice among leaders in the Roman Church just as my modest survey of mainline Protestant leaders revealed a disconnect that must be overcome if we have any hope of sustaining the vitality and relevance of the Church in the Digital Reformation. If leadership is an expression of conferred, inherent, or assumed authority that enables one person to engage, motivate, or inspire another to belief or action, there is often scant evidence of it in the digital domain from formally recognized lay and ordained leaders in ministry. However, the demographic-formerly-known-as-followers is enacting its own self-authorized and socially reinforced authority as digital leaders and ministers in the service of their own spiritual growth and in informal ministries of encouragement, counsel, and comfort to one another. As is the case with many other phenomena in the newly digitally integrated world, change is being led by the swarm rather than the queen.[2]

Fond though ecclesial executives and other leaders often are of translating corporate models of leadership to religious contexts—especially those which invoke Jesus as the ultimate management exemplar[3]—I would argue strongly that spiritual leadership *in any setting* is very different from that aimed at motivating others to meet financial, administrative, productivity, or other business goals. In the Digital Reformation, such models are not only outdated, but wholly inappropriate to the reality of digital engagement that offers so much promise for the Church.

With this in mind, I would suggest that it is not, as a well-known church communication project insists, that "church marketing sucks," as much as it is that marketing the church sucks.[4] That is, we are not *selling something* to the world that will make more people like us, believe in our story, join our churches. We are trying to *be something* in the world that invites connection and compassion, encourages comfort and healing for those in need, and challenges those in power to use that power in the service of justice and love.

Unlike spiritualized versions of corporate practices focused on the *attainment of goals* (*How can we get more members? How can we increase pledges?*), leadership practices in the Digital Reformation are *practice-based*, focusing on sharing resources—traditions, wisdom, kindness, time—that nurture, enhance, and sustain relationships which, in turn, gather themselves into community. Even for individual leaders, leadership is tied not to personal qualities so much as it is to social communication practices. This is why, in fact, the geeks who were often just one snorting laugh away from a wedgie in high school are now pretty much ruling the world.

As a practice, then, digital leadership is fluid, distributed, and more often than not, collective rather than individual. Thus, the awkward embrace of social media by the Vatican, like the absence of religious leaders in the worldwide spiritual response to the rescue of the Chilean miners, and, as we'll see in Chapter 9, techno-tricked-out Evangelical websites, all express a basic inability to minister and provide leadership within an emerging digital habitus characterized largely by networked collaboration and improvisational use of available spiritual resources by groups of people practicing leadership together. Corporate leadership approaches aimed at motivating *others* to meet *your goals* won't be much help here.

Reviewing Reformation: Communication Practices for Leadership

To review, the social communication practices of the Digital Reformation break down, in contrast to mass media communication practices of the broadcast media age, something like this:

KEY CHARACTERISTICS OF MODERN MASS MEDIA COMMUNICATION	KEY CHARACTERISTICS OF DIGITAL SOCIAL MEDIA COMMUNICATION
• One-to-many	• One-to-one-to-one-to-two-to-fifty-to-three-to-five-thousand-to-two-to-one-to-nineteen . . .
• More is better	• Less is often more
• One-directional, top-down	• Multi-directional, networked
• Passive consumers	• Active, creative participants
• Anonymous consumers and producers	• Interactive producers and redistributors
• Communication is mediated by charismatic personalities who invite fantasies of connectedness	• Communication is facilitated by whoever creates or distributes a compelling idea that connects people to others on- and offline
• Consumer interest is correlated to purchasing behavior—success is measured by how much people buy *after* receiving a message	• Participant interest is correlated to distribution—success is indicated by how much people share and elaborate *as* they are receiving a message

KEY CHARACTERISTICS OF MODERN MASS MEDIA COMMUNICATION *cont.*	KEY CHARACTERISTICS OF DIGITAL SOCIAL MEDIA COMMUNICATION *cont.*
• The way to impact purchasing behavior is to offer captivating entertainment and then to interrupt it with a commercial message	• The way to impact participation is by developing engaging content, effectively sharing it with others, and inviting them to comment and collaborate
• Flash, sizzle, and pop capture consumers' attention	• Flash, sizzle, and pop distract participants from meaningful content and conversation

The characteristics of communication through digital social media challenge practices anchored in top-down, institutionally sanctioned authority. They privilege the experience and insights of participants with the most engaging content and most effective practices of interpersonal dialogue. For these reasons, lots of religious leaders have had difficulty integrating digital engagement into their ministries, and this tends to diminish their authority and leadership impact in the Digital Reformation.

Speaking very generally, in the case of Roman Catholic leaders, this follows from a magisterial structure of communication in which, theoretically at least, messages descend through the church hierarchy from the pope, to his bishops, to their priests, and, finally, to the laity. The archetypal image of this process is the pope standing on the balcony of St. Peter's Basilica in Rome, arms raised, blessing the throngs of gathered, anonymous faithful in the square. Often the shot is taken from behind the pope, the crowd extended through the square to the horizon in the background, to illustrate, we may assume, the universal range of his message.

In theological terms, it is perhaps ironic that similar practices are often employed by Evangelical and non-denominational Protestants, whose approach to communication is shaped not by a broad institutional hierarchy, but by traditions that evoke and reinforce communication practices focused on and emanating from individual, charismatic leaders. Though Roman Catholics, outside of mega-events focused on the pope, have not enjoyed quite the success with broadcast media that non-mainline Protestant leaders have found, both draw from practices of church that have made engagement with the one-to-many format of broadcast communication much easier. But these same characteristics have turned out to present challenges to entering the digital domain *on its own terms*.

The digital challenge for mainline Protestant leaders, however, is different. Here, difficulty engaging digital social media may well be amplified by a way of holding leadership comparatively lightly in relation to lay believers and seekers. These practices have developed in no small measure out of our Reformation history and habitus as these have been reshaped in the context of foundational American religious and political experiences. Reforming this habitus in the Digital Reformation is certainly a hefty challenge. But the good news is that the same history and the matrix of practices it shaped prepare mainline church leaders to engage new digital social media with a particular effectiveness that both reinforces and extends core mainline Protestant theologies. To look forward, then, we would again do well to start by looking back.

Back to the Future:
How the Premodern Reformation Shapes the Digital Reformation

At the risk of offering a nutshell summary of Reformation theologies that glosses over a whole raft of important nuances and denominational distinctions, the early churches of the Reformation—Lutheran, Anglican, Reformed (Presbyterian, Congregational)—were responding to what they saw as shortcomings of the Roman Church. Specifically, they objected to practices that separated believers from the means to salvation (the grace of Christ alone, *sola gratia*), which they saw as justified by a believer's faith alone (*sola fide*), without mediation from any human person, whether priest, bishop, or pope. They believed that this understanding of salvation was made clear in the Bible, which alone (*sola scriptura*) was the authoritative source of Christian doctrine, apart from any institutional teachings. In relying on biblical teaching to articulate an understanding of salvation justified through faith by the grace of God in Christ, the reformers sought to call the Church back to what they understood as its roots in the Gospels and their enactment in community as this was articulated in the writings of Paul.

Unlike later political and social critics in France and the British colonies, they did not see their project in revolutionary terms. As I noted earlier, they were not interested in replacing one version of Christianity with another, but in returning to what they saw as a more authentic practice of Christian faith. In many respects, even in their protest against the authority of the Roman Church, they were drawing on an ancient and medieval *habitus* characterized by obedience and a general disdain for novelty. Indeed, when leaders of the brutal German Peasants' War that erupted in 1524 drew on emerging notions of religious freedom, Martin Luther sharply rebuked the rebels and their leaders in the not very subtly titled tract "Against the Robbing and Murdering Hordes of Peasants," which, unfortunately for Luther's popular reputation at the time, printers separated from an earlier "Admonition to Peace" with which he had wished to have it published. Through the European and English Reformations, Calvinist appeals to order and Anglican insistence on uniformity in religious practice likewise tempered revolutionary fervor.[5]

The Same, But Different: Reformation Leadership History

Reformers rather than revolutionaries, then, early Protestants carried much of the ecclesiological structure of the medieval Roman church into new denominations. They reinforced the distinction between clergy and laity on vocational terms, for example, and continued to define the built church as the center of Christian worship. The centrality of individual freedom in Reformation understandings of salvation actually made it all the more important that a well-trained clergy preach, teach, and celebrate worship in believers' native languages. The church as institution and the ordained ministries were needed to provide the education, guidance, and correction believers required to profess their faith, live virtuous lives, and repent of wrongdoing that might close the gates of heaven to them.

At the same time, the concept of the "universal priesthood" articulated by Martin Luther in 1520—"the priesthood of all believers," as it is usually called today—offered a biblically grounded check on the hierarchical structure of the Reformation churches that had been found wanting in medieval Roman Catholicism. If a believer's faith in Jesus Christ was alone required for access to salvation, Luther argued, though different Christians might have different callings in life, the salvation offered by the grace of Christ through faith could render no one believer inherently superior to another. No bishop or priest or monk or nun or anchorite or mystic or hermit—not even the pope himself—could possibly claim to have a more "spiritual" life than those engaged in "secular" vocations. "For all Christians whatsoever really and truly belong to the religious class," Luther insisted, "and there is no difference among them except in so far as they do different work."[6]

This foundational Reformation theology contributed to a mainline Protestant ecclesiology that, on the one hand, maintained a structure of clergy and laity distinguished by their differing vocations and, on the other, invited the development of practices of church that included the participation of various categories of believers in worship and governance. At least in theory, in the Reformation model of church, no one person—a pope, for instance, or a particular pastor—could emerge as *the* decisive voice for the community of believers, even though a priest or bishop might speak *on behalf* of a congregation. According to Reformation theologian Diane V. Bowers, pastor of St. James Lutheran Church in San Leandro, California:

> Of the three—Episcopalians, Lutherans, and the Reformed—it is the Reformed tradition that has incorporated the equality of the community of believers most consistently into its ecclesiological structure. The Presbyterian *Book of Order* both shapes and reflects their identity. It outlines a structure of elections, rules, and rule by committee—committees in which the pastor has no more authority than lay members. This allows Presbyterians to conduct their business "decently and in good order."

Other Reformation traditions have likewise embedded a commitment to balanced lay and clerical participation in structures of governance. The representative model of governance in the

Episcopal Church today, for example, parallels the structure of civil government that was developing in America at the same time, although individual congregations and their clergy owe obedience to their bishops. Nonetheless, Mark Hollingsworth, Bishop of the Episcopal Diocese of Ohio, has argued that the involvement of all believers in the whole life of the church is central to the identity of Episcopalians. "We believe God makes decisions in the life of the church in the pews," he insists, "not just through those of us wearing the purple shirts."[7]

The largest body of Lutheran churches in America (and the largest of the Reformation denominations), the Evangelical Lutheran Church in America (ELCA), likewise follows a representative model of governance while retaining elected bishops with administrative and juridical authority. "The Lutheran Church's governing structure reflects its commitment to the priesthood of all believers and the equality of vocations. Nowhere is this theology made more clear than in our understanding of the role of the pastor," explains Bowers. "A pastor is called by the Holy Spirit and the community to do particular work—teaching, preaching, and administering the sacraments. This work is different, but not more important, than the work carried out by other members of the universal priesthood. Lutherans believe ordination is an office, not a sacrament."

Word Up!: Evangelical Leadership History

By contrast, the churches we have come to know as Evangelical or non-denominational developed not in response to Roman Catholicism, but out of critiques of what their adherents saw as the shortcomings of the Reformation churches. English Puritans, for instance, felt that the Church of England had not gone far enough in separating itself from the episcopal structure of the Roman church, its sacramental system, and "superstitious" practices of worship. For their part, German, Swiss, and other continental Pietists and Anabaptists disputed Lutheran and Calvinist interpretations of scripture and objected to the continuing use of Roman liturgical practices. All of the Reformation churches highlighted the importance of preaching by a well-trained clergy as critical to the education of a laity responsible for making their own claim to the salvation offered by Christ through their profession of faith. But for Puritans, Pietists, Anabaptists, Methodists, and other dissenters from the Reformation churches, the "ministry of the Word"—the reading of scripture and the pastor's interpretation in the sermon— was the central element of worship. It connected believers to the Bible and provided learned interpretation that supported the living out of biblical faith in daily life.

Moreover, because dissenting Protestants were, well, dissenters, they did not have conventional access to the educational resources and vocational discernment processes used to identify and develop leaders in the mainline churches. Their early leadership was determined, then, not through institutional assessment and hierarchical ascent, but through the active expression of their spiritual intellect and pastoral expertise in communities. A minister could come to claim authority in a community precisely because his—or more rarely, her—gifts in preaching and pastoral care drew believers into a particular formation of church. Indeed, the development of the Evangelical tradition in late-nineteenth and early-twentieth century America is often marked by a more entrepreneurial approach to ministry leadership that carries directly into the present day. This practice continues extensively today in the "emerging church" movement, which often develops out of the homiletic, pastoral, and organizational strengths of a particular leader (who in many cases is sponsored by an institutional church) at least as much as out of grassroots gatherings of believers and seekers.

Calls to ministry in Evangelical, non-denominational, and other non-mainline churches, therefore, developed and remain closely tied to personal charisma. From the earliest days, charismatic preaching established both the spiritual and intellectual authority of the pastor and the distinctiveness of his role. Indeed, the Puritan leader Richard Baxter suggested that the effective preacher say at least one thing in every sermon that no one in the congregation could understand in order to reinforce the greater learning of the clergy and make clear that not everyone is called to the ministry of the Word.[8]

The History of the Future:
Why Historical Practice Matters in the Digital Reformation

Again, I am oversimplifying a long and complex church history here. But it is fair to say that one effect of the different histories, theologies, and ecclesiologies of mainline and non-mainline Protestant churches has been the development of distinct, recognizable styles of communication, leadership, and community. Very generally speaking, in non-mainline churches, communication is directed from and responds to a single, charismatic leader who is the center of a worship experience focused on preaching that extends to the community. This way of practicing church has allowed non-mainline churches significantly greater success, measured both by broadcast audience and local membership, with radio and television, which operate out of communication models that are congenial to traditional Evangelical leadership structures.

Non-mainline religious groups have so far had a far greater presence on the internet, too. But they have tended to follow a broadcast model of one-to-many communication, however sophisticated their digital enhancements might be. This has allowed them to "feast on the flock," reinforcing their views and supporting disbursed members of their communities. Despite the resources poured into new media communication, social media engagement by Evangelical and non-denominational churches has not generally invited an extension of their ministries beyond their own traditional constituencies.[9]

Digital social media, however, function within a habitus that is new in the realm of electronic communications, but which has significant overlaps with the practices of church and associated styles of communication that emerged from the distinctive histories of the Reformation churches. The habitus of the Digital Reformation thus creates the opportunity for mainline churches to meld practices of collaborative improvisation at the grassroots level with ministries enacted through practices of listening, attentiveness, connection, and engagement. As we'll see in the next chapter, the general leadership style of mainline Christianity allows us to move beyond broadcast messaging to genuine social communication supported by relational leadership and distributed authority.

This reconfiguration of authority creates obvious challenges for leaders in ministry, but it doesn't mean that leadership goes away. Its practice, however, does require considerable reformation if we want to make the most of the opportunities presented by new digital media to meaningfully share the Good News of God's love and justice with an ever more closely networked world. Of course, this does require that leaders in ministry take practices of digital leadership as seriously as they do other elements of their vocations. As we've learned, applying broadcast-based practices will not help mainline leaders to make the most of the opportunities for education, evangelism, community-building, and pastoral care in general that are available in the Digital Reformation. Neither will attempting to wait out what is no mere trend, but rather a profound cultural change.

———

As we move on to consider renewed practices of leadership for the Digital Reformation in Chapter 8 and in the case studies in Chapter 9, it is worthwhile to reflect on where your congregation stands in the leadership mix. How distributed is leadership among all members, and how much is it focused on clergy? In what areas would greater involvement of rank-and-file members of churches—people who have perhaps never been actively involved in formal leadership or administration—enrich the practice of leadership? Where might such distributed involvement create friction or otherwise challenge the practice of leadership as it stands today? In a new world in which crossing borders and sharing authority is more important than ever, how can you imagine employing the tools of social media to both loosen boundaries and reinforce them?

8

LEADERSHIP IS A PLACE

Practicing Church in the Digital Village

You're not a leader, you're a place. You're like a park or a garden. If it's comfortable and cool, people are attracted.

—*Joi Ito*

I imagine Bruce Robison on one of those old-fashioned bikes—the kind with a basket on the front and a bell that goes brrrr-ring, brrrr-ring, brrrr-ring. In my mind's eye, he's dressed like a nineteenth-century parson just come from morning prayer, black cassock waving behind him as he wheels over cobblestone streets to visit Mrs. Dunby, who has been uncharacteristically absent the last three mornings. It could be her arthritis acting up, he thinks. Or, perhaps it's the cold going around that's punctuated the homily with sniffles and coughs the past couple weeks. In any case, it's not like Lily Dunby to miss Morning Prayer, so Father Bruce pedals toward the park, waving to the gaggle of old guys drinking coffee and gossiping at a table outside the local café.

When this scene plays out in my head, it is always autumn in the neighborhood where the thick-stoned St. Andrew's Episcopal Church serves as a reminder of the more upscale history of Pittsburgh's Highland Park neighborhood, dotted as it once was with the small estates of the Carnegie-Frick-Mellon set. I see gold and scarlet leaves floating from the trees as families stroll down the avenue after Sunday services. For a very long time, though—certainly through all of Robison's nearly twenty-year tenure there—the neighborhood's been on somewhat harder times, a victim of the collapse of the steel industry in the seventies and one downturn after another in the years since then. It's still a lovely neighborhood, but it's more urban now, a little grittier, more working class with an artsy, yuppie edge. And on the early February day I talked with Robison, there were no fluttering leaves. The whole city was feet-deep in snow that had kept almost everyone from church on Sunday and everything else through most of the week.

Still, Robison brought the Herbert-esque fantasy to mind himself as we talked about his use of social media in his ministry. "You know, the church used to be the center of a town or a village," Robison said. "A priest helped to keep people connected with each other in that community in very practical ways that went beyond the Sunday service. The priest was an active presence in the community, not someone just 'over there,' in that building we go to on Sunday."

St. Andrew's functions as center for much of the civic, educational, and cultural activity in the neighborhood, making the church present as an engaged member of the wider community. For Robison, blogging and being active on Facebook enables him to be that presence in a neighborhood like Highland Park, where changed patterns of work, family, and faith—not to mention the periodic blizzard—often amplify separateness over connection. Robison, like so many other clergy and lay leaders, posts his sermons and offers other commentary on a blog, a practice he sees as valuable in particular for the many older adults in the congregation. But his day-to-day engagements take a more minimalist form by way of Facebook.

Unlike other leaders who use Facebook in the context of their ministry, Robison is the soul of brevity in his own posts. Between periodic updates on the Steelers and the long-suffering Pirates, he posts things like, "@ our diocesan clergy conference . . ." or "Great morning at St. Andrew's . . ." more than he offers reflection, opinion, or information. True, there are periodic announcements of church events and a note once in a while on something he's recently read. But the real energy of Robison's engagement on Facebook is elsewhere. He is, I would suggest, one of the Great Attenders of the Digital Reformation, the evidence of which is not his laconic status updates and posts but the number of times his wall reads "Bruce commented on [someone's] status" or "Bruce wrote on [someone's] wall." More than almost anyone in my Facebook world, Robison seems to take particular care not just to draw people into conversations he initiates on his Facebook page, but to visit the pages of people in his network and participate in their conversations or comment on the things they've seen as sufficiently interesting to post on their walls.

A parishioner announces her safe arrival in Rome. Robison notices. Another shares news that she's headed home from a hospital stay. Robison sends blessings. Yet another is heading to the doctor for tests. More blessings. A colleague shares a presentation. Robison thanks him. It's your birthday? Expect a greeting from Robison. Little bit by little bit, Robison attends to the lives of members of his church, friends, family, and colleagues as they share news from the mundane to the mournful. It all matters to him. "I just can't see everyone as much as I would want to," Robison explains. "But I can pay attention to what they're posting on Facebook, so I have at least some sense of what's happening in people's lives."

He takes particular care to connect to young adults in his congregation as they head off to college. "You know, lots of these kids grew up in the church. They were acolytes. They were active in youth group," says Robison. He continues,

> Then they go off to college, and we only see them on breaks. Maybe. It used to be the case that they would often just fade away from the church. Or, maybe the church faded away from them. Now I can be more aware of what's happening while they're at school. And, because so many people in the congregation are also on Facebook, we can all continue to be a community for them when they are home for Christmas or over the summer. We don't have to say much for them to know we're still here, that they continue to be important to us.

Abba, Give Me a Tweet:
Micro-Wisdom for the Digital Reformation

In his Facebook interactions Robison offers a balance of listening and attentiveness that is particularly meaningful in the Digital Reformation. His is a digital ministry of presence that blends something of the pastoral practice idealized in George Herbert's *The Country Parson* with the wisdom practice exemplified by the desert Abbas and Ammas, early Christian monastics who took refuge in the deserts outside of Egypt, Syria, Turkey, and Persia (present-day Iran) in the third and fourth century. These Desert Mothers (Ammas) and Fathers (Abbas) were renowned for the depth of spiritual wisdom they doled out to disciples and more casual seekers in memorable morsels that could be shared with others. The Ammas and Abbas are ancient tweet-masters who remind us that, as theologian and blogger Susan Thistlethwaite has insisted, "Just because something is short, doesn't mean it has to be stupid."[1]

Beyond this, their less-is-more communication practices assumed that everything that might be known about a particular concern need not be said, that wisdom was not a prize to be handed over but a journey that could be encouraged with as little as a thoughtful nudge. Simply attending quietly to those who sought them out for brief or extended instruction and formation and offering a small "word"—a little more than a tweet, usually, but less than a blog post—helped to keep Christians coping with changes in ancient society connected to the roots of their faith.

While we tend to think of desert ascetics as isolated from the mainstream of society, their relative closeness to at least smaller trading centers made them accessible to the many people who sought their teaching. Typically, the Abbas and Ammas lived a day or so by foot from a small village or town so that they could sell the baskets and other hand goods they crafted to sustain their simple lives. The back and forth of monks and pilgrims was very much a part of the spirituality of the ancient desert. But it was hardly the whole of it.

The customary form of address to an Amma or Abba was the center of an engaged, but closely managed, spirituality. "Amma, give me word," a seeker would ask a wise woman. But this "word" was no simple mantra or the sort of "sacred word" repeated over and over that is familiar to centering prayer practitioners. What we refer to now as an Amma's or Abba's "word" is a very loose translation of the Greek *rhema*, which "had a similar connotation of a deed or an 'event' which is announced by a word," according to Christian spirituality scholar Douglas Burton-Christie. "It expresses both the close relation between life and action that characterized these words as well as the weight and authority they possessed."[2]

The "words" of the Ammas and Abbas were thus expressions of a more extensive Christian habitus, a life practice that integrated the concerns and needs of a particular person with the deeper experience of Christian faith. While we would misunderstand the meaning of *rhema* by assuming the Ammas and Abbas were functioning as blank conduits for the literal word of God to a seeker, the words offered by the sages were believed to be inspired by God. In this sense, they were, like micro-versions of Paul's letters, expressions of the desert sage's profound listening to the seeker in light of the wisdom attained through a lifetime of devotion to God.

I always have an itch to dive into these sayings as into a bowl of trick-or-treat candy, picking out the Snickers bar gems (Abba Poemen said, "Vigilance, self-knowledge, and discernment: these are the guides to the soul") and leaving the root beer barrels (he also said, "All bodily comfort is an abomination to the Lord") for the next kid.[3] But the point of the words offered by the wise men and women of the desert is that they spoke from attentiveness to a particular life and toward the growth of this life as it participated in the fullness of the Body of Christ. It is the situatedness of the wisdom of the Ammas and Abbas that motivated their followers to collect their words into volumes of sayings that they could share with others. We might call these collections the first great trending, global "retweets" of the Christian tradition, turning up as they did from Ethiopia to Ireland in the early centuries of the church because they were both memorable and meaningful in the context of Christian practice.

The words of the desert Abbas and Ammas offered lived wisdom for lived spiritual practice. Unlike modern models of leadership—however benevolent or spiritually centered—"leadership" as it was practiced by the Ammas and Abbas was not about *influencing* believers to act in one way or another. They weren't, that is, motivational speakers. Rather, they practiced ministries of listening and attentiveness. Devotees were meant to mull on their teachings, not to obey them in the context of institutionalized church practice *per se*. So, however much common worship, the periodic agape meal, and a Eucharist now and then might have benefited the growth of an early Christian's soul, we never see in the sayings of the Desert Mothers and Fathers things that pop up every day on my churchy Twitter feed (a random selection):

> "Preaching at St. Cecelia's this Sunday!"
>
> "Youth gathering tonight at Queen Bean Coffees and Teas."
>
> "My 'all saints' sermon is now on the church website."
>
> "U2-Charist this Sat. @ All Souls!"
>
> "Check out my new blog post!"

You get the idea. I'm certainly as guilty as the next tweeter, but, really, the string of self- (or church-) referential "important" things we all have to announce makes me think I should perhaps be following Amma Matrona a little more closely: "We carry ourselves wherever we go and we cannot escape temptation by mere flight."

Who was she talking to? Who was trying to run away from her- or himself all the way to the seemingly dry and empty desert, unable even there to find a sufficient measure of self-understanding that would permit a fuller turning toward God? Amma Matrona said, "Many people living secluded lives on the mountain have perished by living like people in the world. It is better to live in a crowd and want to live a solitary life than to live a solitary life but all the time be longing for company."[4]

People turned to the desert Ammas and Abbas because they exemplified lives of simplicity and Christ-centeredness that many believed the rapidly institutionalizing Church was trading in for greater social respectability and political influence in the late Roman Empire. Even as Paul was writing in the first century, many scholars argue, he was struggling to encourage, on the one hand, an embrace of the radical egalitarianism of the Gospels and, on the other, an accommodation to the local culture that would allow young Christian communities a measure of security and safety. Many of the objectionable passages in his authentic letters and in those believed to have been written in his name latter seem to scholars to reflect this desire to "go along to get along." This tension between accommodation and transformation would certainly seem to be one of the more durable elements of the basic habitus of Christian life.

By the early fourth century, after the conversion of the emperor Constantine, Christians were enjoying a newfound social and political acceptance that often caused them to turn away from their more marginalized roots toward the trappings that came with imperial status. The move to the desert by Christian monks was a rejection of this compromised Christianity, and the pilgrimages of all manner of Christians to monastic communities and solitary hermits in the desert were part of an often pained effort to remember more authentic Christian selves and communities. Amma Syncletica kept it simple, then. "Salvation is exactly this," she said, "the twofold love of God and of our neighbor."[5]

The between-the-lines of the collections of sayings of the desert Ammas and Abbas seems, then, to be a desire to be seen both as we are in the complexity of daily life *and* as we would like to be as Christians who are attentive to the spiritual nuances of that life.

Listening to the Digital Reformation:
It's Not All About "Getting the Word Out"

This brings us to what is the grand irony of the overlap between the Broadcast Age and the Digital Reformation: the people who are best at this kind of knowing today are not, to any meaningful degree, spiritual exemplars or leaders in ministry, but rather advertisers. The people who are attending to what I do online every day—what I read, what videos I watch, what I share with my friends and "friends," how I shop, what words appear again and again in my tweets and status updates—for the most part want to sell me something. And, they know better than to do that by focusing on what they have to offer in itself. They know I'll be more in a mood to buy if what they have to sell connects to something of meaning in my life. Better still if it has something to do with an identity to which I aspire. I'm not suggesting here that we become better advertisers for our churches. But I do think we now have the capability and at least some of the wherewithal to listen to believers and seekers at least as attentively as do the marketing staff at Apple or Macy's.

Every once in a while one of my friends will post a little screed about the Facebook ads that show up to the right of their profile page. It usually goes something like this: "What could I possibly have written that would make FB think I would want to vote for X, buy a book on 'spiritual warfare,' or lose twenty pounds this weekend?" If we get annoyed when the Facebook advertising automatons don't know us well enough, imagine how it feels when our priest or pastor keeps posting or tweeting stuff that betrays no understanding of who we are or who we hope to be. Listening, attending, connecting, and engaging on social networking sites comes down not to talking *about* yourself, but to talking *as* yourself about things that matter to those in your network. This is exactly the practice so richly exemplified by the dessert Ammas and Abbas.

Random Acts of Reformation:
Meaningful Digital Engagement, In Particular

Marc Andrus, the Bishop of the Episcopal Diocese of California, got this attentive engagement exactly right for me not long ago. In the wee hours of his birthday, which I'd noted because Facebook reminded me—a technological grace that allows almost everyone in the Digital Reformation to celebrate the nativity of almost everyone else—I jotted a quick greeting. A few minutes later, I had a note back from Bishop Andrus, thanking me for my greetings and, more, giving me a bit of a "word" on an article I'd recently written.

I don't know Marc well, so it was a surprise that he had something beyond polite niceties to say back to me (which would have been lovely in itself), something that said he was actually paying attention to the particularity of my life. What's more, I learned from other folks in a loose configuration of Episcopalians that he had done this same sort of thing with scads of folks who'd wished him well on his birthday, connecting the reality of his incarnation to theirs, the relationship stretching well beyond the virtual to the deeply spiritually real.

There's one final element to my tiny exchange with Bishop Andrus that seems worth our notice, too. As I mentioned, we don't know one another well. We've met a few times. He knows a bit about my work. He's been kind and supportive on a number of occasions, but our interactions have been limited to our respective professional domains. It's not as if we hang out together. It's not as if I would know when his birthday is if he weren't my Facebook "friend." Our birthday interaction, then, wasn't exactly random, but almost.

Yet for the Abbas and Ammas, much more deeply personal spiritual exchanges with seekers were almost entirely random. A pilgrim showed up at the door, and ancient customs of hospitality dictated that she or he be made welcome, given food and wine, a mat for sleeping. The sage would listen and observe as the guest settled in and shared her story. "Give me a word," the seeker would ask, and the Amma or Abba would oblige, not out of a commitment to personal relationship—most of the visitors to an Abba's or Amma's cell never returned—but out of a commitment to an ideal of Christian relatedness that sees us all as God's children, each worthy of attention and care. Out of something of that same commitment, those who sought out the Ammas and Abbas would share the wisdom they'd gleaned from their visit to the desert with others on their journey back to the towns and cities of early Christendom and in the complicated lives to which they returned. The authority of their wisdom was shared, so their spiritual leadership was widely distributed.

I see the digital translation of this ancient practice for leaders in ministry today playing out something like this: When we're active in social media sites like Twitter and Facebook, all sorts of people we know a little and lots of people we don't know at all connect with us. They do this for a variety of reasons, the nut of most of these being that people want to be seen and known by someone whom they perceive as having meaningful spiritual insight to share in relation to their own lives. They're standing outside our digital cells, waiting to be invited in just as they are. They're not interested in a "leader" in the modern sense—someone who will influence them, however benevolently, to think or do one thing or another. They're interested in someone who leads with compassionate welcome, someone who provides space to experience something of the divine in themselves, and who offers a word or two to encourage that search and the life practices it prompts.

When we're under the sway of a broadcast mindset, however, we think in terms of billboards rather than birthday cards. We think every word we share in the digital domain has to directly inspire each and every person who might encounter it. It doesn't. Indeed, it works so much better when it doesn't, when we use the new medium to grow particular relationships that connect to other particular relationships. Tending seedlings in the Digital Reformation is at least as important as sowing seeds.

The desert Ammas and Abbas understood that the ancient equivalent of a super-sized Christianity wasn't working for them or for lots of other believers, so they retreated to the desert or the mountains. But, while they craved a certain measure of solitude and quiet, they were hardly alone in the wilderness. Rather, they were cultivating a renewal of a kind of relational particularity that we are absolutely able to do when we attend carefully to even a handful of Twitter followers or Facebook friends before we attempt to offer any sort of "word."

The Ammas and Abbas teach us that when we resist the go-tell-it-on-the-mountain broadcast urge in an abundantly fertile medium, we have the opportunity to facilitate the sharing not of a narrow Christian *message*, but an expansive Christian *practice* with a whole host of people, known and unknown to us. In the Digital Reformation, that practice is increasingly enacted in social media locales. As Bishop Andy Doyle insists, "The social media community is a place—a spiritual place. And in doing the work I do on Twitter and Facebook, I am in the midst of that." Being in that place—just listening to and being attentive to others there—is as important as any message we might offer.

Creating digital space as spiritual space can change relationships profoundly. In the course of researching and writing this book, I talked with dozens of people about their use of new social media in the context of ministry and religious practice more generally. Every single one of them talked about the ways in which having a context for more regular engagement with others in the spiritual life enriched and extended their relationships. Kirk Smith, for instance, maintains that his use of digital media has "created a whole different world in terms of relationships with people" in his diocese. "In the old days," he says, "people would see the bishop once a year—if that. Now they see me every day. More importantly, I see them. We know each other in ways that just would not have been possible in the past. And this is true not just for me, of course. It makes clergy more accessible. It makes people in congregations more accessible to each other."

Keith Anderson, pastor of the Lutheran Church of the Redeemer in Woburn, Massachusetts, highlights the continuity between digital and face-to-face interaction:

> So many of the conversations I have at church these days start with, "Oh, I saw on Facebook that you did this or that." This medium is so real to us now. It sparks our interest. It sparks conversation. It helps us to connect online and offline. More and more, it's integrated into our lives together. It's where people are, and that's where we have to be if we want to be relevant and meaningful as a church.

Location, Location, Location: Leadership as Digital Locale

We don't typically think of the desert caves and hovels of fourth-century monastics as parts of this kind of networked space, but they absolutely were. On the margins of an emerging urban Christianity of increasing social and political complexity, the desert communities functioned as connective and restorative spaces that drew people out of the fray of city life and enabled them to reenter it with renewed understandings of themselves and the faith that would sustain them in the changing church and world. The particular wisdom of the Ammas and Abbas was central to that experience, but no less than the locale itself, which encouraged the attentiveness to self, other, and God that grounded the sages' "words." And, as the

Ammas and Abbas made clear, this locale was expressed more in the metaphor of the desert, than in the physical reality of it.

"Let us seek after the desert, not only that of the place, but also that of disposition," wrote John Chrysostom. Like the Abbas and Ammas of the desert, the fourth-century archbishop of Constantinople, himself known as one of the "great communicators" of the early church, modeled a version of ascetic leadership that would invite believers to create sacred space in the course of active lives.[6] He understood, on the one hand, that we need to set apart space and time to nurture our relationship to God and other in the context of the believing community. On the other hand, Chrysostom's own multifaceted life was testimony for the need for alternative spiritual spaces within the context of ordinary lives that help believers and seekers remain connected—or develop connections—to the communities that enrich, sustain, and challenge their faith.

When we undertake leadership as a practice of Christian presence in social media landscapes where believers spend nearly a quarter of their online time[7]—nearly seven hours a month on Facebook alone[8]—we are contributing to the creation of a networked sacred space not unlike that which the Ammas and Abbas carved out of the ancient desert. We are allowing ourselves to stroll or pedal along the various paths and avenues that connect the widely distributed outposts of the new digital global village. What if those who might be seeking spiritual engagement in your community started hanging out right outside the doors of your church. Would you squander that opportunity? Wouldn't you at least invite folks in to chat with you and with one another for a bit?

Leveraging this networked accessibility and the degree to which it deepens our knowledge of one another is the root of effective leadership in the Digital Reformation. Indeed, to the extent that personal charisma or institutional status still do matter in the Church, it is largely through their ability to gather people together into informal communities where they can express their own ideas, engage with others, and collectively shape new realities in which all involved have a personal investment. It is in this sense that Joi Ito, a technology entrepreneur and social activist, described leadership in the Digital Age as "a place."

Ito was actively involved in the 2004 Howard Dean presidential campaign, which demonstrated one of the first notably effective uses of digital locales as sites for collaborative social exchange.[9] The power of this practice was extended exponentially in Barack Obama's 2008 campaign. Cannily using text messages, Facebook pages, and Twitter feeds of both the campaign itself and supporters configured in a wide range of groupings, the Obama team was able to provide a vast space for supporters to share their perspectives on the issues at play in the election. This level of participation in the wider political conversation—participation that was meaningful to millions of people who had felt marginalized in previous elections—generated a level of enthusiasm for the candidate and politics itself that hadn't been seen for generations. The simple practice of providing a safe space for engagement changed the shape of American politics, precisely because it changed the experience of leadership and of relationship among those would have in the past understood themselves as passive followers consuming messages from above. In the Obama campaign, supporters felt that they had a real part to play in the campaign.

Keeping It Real in the Digital Reformation: Consistency in Digital Leadership

Of course, once the Obama campaign was over, we were also able to learn some lessons associated with presenting inconsistent practices of leadership within and outside digital communities. That is, while creating space for active, engaged participation across constituencies was a top priority for the Obama campaign, the challenges of governance once the election was won understandably reordered priorities for the administration. By the midterm elections of 2010, many younger voters in particular felt alienated from the president whom they had come out in droves to elect two years earlier.

There are lots of reasons for this, certainly, and it's not the purpose of this book to sort them out. But we can fairly say that at least one part of the equation was a shift in leadership practice—arguably, one demanded by the very different roles of candidate and president—that left many voters feeling voiceless and displaced once President Obama was in office. The lesson here for leaders in ministry is that there is not one mode of communication and leadership in the church in a social media space and another in the physical and institutional spaces of the church. Practices of listening, attending, connecting, and engaging that characterize effective digital ministry have to be consistently applied in both digital and face-to-face ministries.

"The surprising thing about digital media, I think," says Keith Anderson, "is how humanizing it is." He continues:

> We just see so much more of each other's whole lives than ever before. It really matters that we do this well, that we put care into how we're now connecting with people in our churches across the board. Being consistent is really key. Being real, and open, and as human we can be wherever we are, is key. It's not like you're this different person online than you are in church. I think social media are absolutely teaching us how to be so much better about this in every aspect of our ministries, in every part of the church.

Anderson's "keep it real" advice sounds simple enough on the surface. But it extends well beyond just "being yourself" in digital environments, though that certainly is necessary. Rather, "keeping it real" in the Digital Reformation means really creating church as a network of spaces—digital and physical, liturgical and social—to which people can come to express, nurture, and, in the context of relationships with others, transform the reality of their own experience in more positive ways. For Anderson, these spaces are as likely to be at the local coffeehouse, the neighborhood pub, a bowling alley, or on his Facebook page as he invites people to wrestle a sermon with him, as they are in the church "proper." In this way, he practices a flexible, improvisational ministry of presence that invites engagement, participation, and collaboration across a multidimensional spiritual space.

You've Got to Get Out More Often: Toward Convergent Ministries

The presence Anderson, Robison, and other new digital ministers have modeled in their social media practice is much more than church marketing or pastoral gesture. This digital ministry crystallizes the most central practice of Christian faith—love of neighbor—by offering genuine warmth, a measure of wisdom, and meaningful witness that both connects and extends Christian community. Have we perfected this digital leadership practice yet? Certainly not. There are lots of ways for leaders to nurture and extend the relationships we're developing in social media contexts.

One way is suggested by a convergence of some of the digital ministry practices we've seen so far. Robison's "digital village parson" practice, for instance, highlights the value of traveling off your own Facebook page or Twitter feed to engage with others on their own digital turf. Bishop Kirk Smith's practice of digital witness, discussed in chapter 6, illustrates the relational and moral power of using your Facebook page—especially if you're someone with the sort of institutional or other status that marks you as more of a "thought leader" in and across communities—as a forum for those on the margins of church and society. So, what if we hopped further off our personal pages, generated conversation, and worked to introduce the concerns of others into the wider conversation? Where would we do that? The sorts of Facebook community pages created by Susan Russell, Ron Pogue, and Chris Yaw are good stopping places for leaders in ministry hoping to nurture community across the wider Church.

These pages are the new coffee shops, cafés, and public squares in which we can begin to cultivate the diverse, geographically expansive, collaborative networks that are the greatest promise of the Digital Reformation. We need to ride our bikes over to these spaces a bit more in our digital ministries if we're going to reach beyond our local communities. Oh, and from the group page that links most naturally to your denomination, diocese, synod, congregation, or other community configuration, it's really only a click or two away to those folks over at the "Progressive Christianity and Spirituality Page," the "Spiritual But Not Religious" group to which many mainline Christians are migrating, or whatever other group connects naturally to your community and extends it.

Keep pedaling from there. Church-sponsored or related charities? Seminaries? Affiliated colleges and universities? Ten minutes of search time on Facebook or Twitter will introduce you to these communities. Follow them. Like them. Listen to them. Share their news on your page by way of introducing them to your friends and followers. Cheer them on. Comment on their posts. In sum, be a good friend and neighbor. And, when you've got something really worth sharing—like, say, you've wrangled a couple busloads of bishops and schlepped them into the heat of the desert and the heart of what may well be "the civil rights issue of our time"— share it in these contiguous digital communities, too.

Once you've travelled more extensively in what has been called the "walled garden" that is Facebook and, to a lesser extent, Twitter, it's worthwhile to look for opportunities to jump the hedge into commentary spaces for mainstream and alternative news sites. As in the past, it still takes an often elusive mix of perceived status, professional connections, and something we could chalk up to grace or luck to get full commentary on the opinion page of the *New York Times* or even your local newspaper. But, more often than not, all it takes to offer a perspective on a news or opinion piece in the digital age is a willingness to create a user account with a news site. Indeed, as online news sites tighten commentary guidelines to reduce hate speech and spam, they are ever more interested in reasoned commentary from thought influencers, especially those who don't mind sharing their names and institutional affiliations. So, the note you wrote to accompany the link to that amazing article from *Religion Dispatches*, the *Guardian* religion section, or *USA Today's* "On Faith" blog? Go ahead and post a version of it on the comment section of these sites, as well. They're more than happy to hear from you. In fact, if you're not a wing nut, they're ecstatic.

There are multiple benefits for leaders in ministry who endeavor to bridge digital manifestations of broadcast media with digital social media practices. First, especially for ministers whose churches or associated organizations have been absent from or unevenly represented in wider media conversations on religion in general and Christianity in particular, offering commentary on mainline news sites broadens the conversation for readers who have come to see such comments as important adjuncts to the news as it is presented. Further, such commentary extends the witness to Christian compassion and advocacy that is often forgotten as a central value in our communities. This, in turn, distinguishes and reforms the image of mainline Christianity in ways that may invite believers who have checked out of our churches and seekers who have not considered them as meaningful sites for spiritual engagement into our communities.

———

Who is standing outside your digital cell right now, waiting for a word? Where might you ride your digital bicycle today, and with what communities could you nurture new relationship? How might you share compassion and welcome in the Digital Reformation? As a ministry leader in the Digital Reformation, how can you enact the kinds of attentiveness and presence that mark the digital domain as a fertile space for spiritual exploration and growth? In the Digital Reformation, our ability to shape and sustain sacred space as fully online as we attempt to do in our churches is central to our ability to build communities that nurture, encourage, and sustain the Church as an enduring site of transformation.

The next chapter looks at two very different churches and three very different leaders in ministry as each takes on the challenges and opportunities of the Digital Reformation. These case studies bring together what we've learned throughout *Tweet If You ♥ Jesus* about communication, community, and leadership through practices of listening, attentiveness, connection, and engagement.

Part V

PRACTICING REFORMATION

9

THROUGH A MIRROR, LESS DIMLY

The Digital Reformation in Practice

For now we see in a mirror, dimly, but then we will see face to face.

—*1 Corinthians 13:12*

Different histories, theologies, and social contexts have shaped different approaches to communication, community, and leadership that are expressed in the websites and the Facebook pages of mainline and Evangelical or non-denominational Protestant churches. In this chapter, we will explore how these differences play out by examining more closely the digital media presences of two churches, Harvest Bible Chapel and Wicker Park Lutheran Church, both in the Chicago area. We'll also look at the Twitter practices of two individual leaders in ministry, those of Harvest Bible Chapel's senior pastor, James MacDonald, and Bishop Andy Doyle of the Episcopal Diocese of Texas.

I should acknowledge at the outset that, while this sort of comparison allows differences to appear in greater relief, it also invites a certain over-characterization of each community that I would generally prefer to avoid. However, because this isn't a book on web design or social media communications and marketing *per se*, I'm going to take the risk of creating a sharper contrast than might appear if we had the space and time to consider the digital self-representations of half a dozen church communities. I should say, too, that I selected the two churches I discuss here not because they represent either the very best or very worst of how churches are communicating with new social media, but precisely because they are situated in the wide middle ground of the digital landscape where we're all still pretty much trying to figure it out.

That said, the website of the Harvest Bible Chapel (*www. harvestbible.org*), a multi-site, non-denominational church based in the Chicago area, is fairly characteristic of the more technically sophisticated non-mainline engagement with digital media. In addition to five Chicago-area locations, Harvest Bible Chapel has forty-three satellite locations across North America and another sixteen overseas. Each location has a separate website that is networked to the main church website that is the main focus of our discussion. A screenshot of a Google search for the church [Figure 1] highlights in the headings of the first five entries not only the name of the church, but the name of the founding pastor, The Reverend Dr. James MacDonald.

The results shown are not an accident of Google searching. The design of every website includes "meta-tags," words or short

Figure 1: A Google search of "Harvest Bible Chapel"

Figure 2: The Harvest Bible Chapel website home page

phrases that let search engines know how to list the site in search results. In most web design programs, the default keyword is the generic name of the page—"Welcome" or "Home Page," for example. But a good web designer will typically edit the default settings so that a more specific search term comes up: "Welcome to St. Whosit Church." A search for "Harvest Bible Church" appears with MacDonald's name, then, because it is specifically designed to do just that. "Harvest Bible Chapel" and "James MacDonald" are equivalent search terms, so a search for one always leads to the other, their intentionally twined digital identities expressing an important reality of lived practice in the church.

The home page of the church's website deepens the identification of the church with the pastor, featuring him twice on a page that loses much of its purple-hued vibrancy in the black-and-white screen shot shown in Figure 2.

In the page heading, the congregation is also shown, but in muted tones, behind the pastor. A bright green "Become a Healthier You" banner scrolls across the page, highlighting an upcoming preaching series by MacDonald. The "Listen to this Week's Message" link connects to an audio recording by MacDonald, which

visitors to the site may listen to online for the current week or purchase for previous weeks.

All of this makes the message clear to the site visitor: Harvest
Bible Chapel *is* James MacDonald, a point sharpened by the audio
messages, videos, blog, Twitter feed, and other professionally
produced digital media featuring MacDonald. Indeed, though the
pages for each of five separate Harvest Bible Chapel "campuses" in
the Chicago area include a picture of the pastor for that location,
these are single-tone images that blend into the background color
for the campus page, and the minister is not named. The body of
the local campuses' pages continues the identification with Mac-
Donald, reflecting a hierachy drawn from the church's reading of
scripture: "The whole focus of Harvest is vertical, not horizontal,"
MacDonald explains on the website. "We know it's God."

Differences in theology and practice notwithstanding, the technical sophistication of websites like these often makes mainline religious leaders throw up their hands in digital despair. But as we've
long known, "all that glitters is not gold." Take the decidedly more
modest digital presence of another Chicago area church, Wicker
Park Lutheran Church (*www.wickerparklutheran.org*), starting with
a Google search for "Wicker Park Chicago," shown in Figure 3.

Figure 3: A Google search for "Wicker Park Lutheran Church"

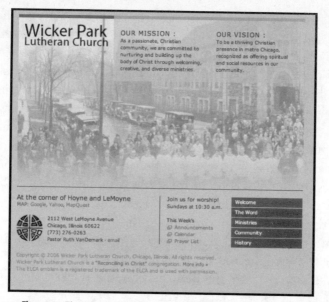

Figure 4: The Wicker Park Lutheran Church website home page

Wicker Park Lutheran has a much smaller website, so fewer pages show up in a Google search. A careful scan of the Google search will reveal that the pastor is The Reverend Ruth VanDemark, but you'll only find her within the body of a listing. Otherwise, the site's meta-tags express the concerns that apparently guided its structuring: welcome, community, and an apparent affection for choral music. Likewise, an outside-in orientation is amplified by the church's listing on the popular community review site Yelp, and by directions to the church.

This orientation is echoed in—it has to be said, alas—what is maybe one of the dowdiest church websites I've come across in a while [Figure 4]. The page itself is a dullish tan, with no color photos, so it loses little in a black-and-white rendering shown here. There are no scrolling flash animations, no links to digital goodies. The design itself (not the content) seems not to have been updated since 2006, which is a lifetime in digital time. Clearly, in a web design contest, Wicker Park Lutheran Church would lose.

But when we consider the story the Wicker Park Lutheran web-page tells, something very different emerges. Okay, it's still frumpy and brown and nothing cool scrolls across the screen when you open it. But the church's pared-down, old-timey webpage nonetheless makes its mission and vision clear, and sets these, by way of turn-of-the-century photograph of the congregation outside the church building, within a historical church community connected to the world outside its doors. The orientation of members of the church community to one another, including the pastor, and to the world outside the church is expressed on the website perhaps without great boldness, but with a subdued conviction nonetheless. It provides meaningful content for those who might want to visit the church without vicariously giving away the goods of face-to-face interaction. It would undoubtedly turn off seekers used to the representational style of denominations with more modern histories, but for those connected to or interested in the mainline churches emerging directly from the Reformation, the Wicker Park Lutheran website says, "We're a lot like you."

I'm going to take a not terribly great risk here, not really knowing either pastor,[1] and say that these differences are not anchored in the personalities of either MacDonald or VanDemark. Self-promoting egomaniacs rise up across all the denominations as do, albeit perhaps to a lesser extent, self-effacing servants of the flock. Neither digital presence shows the respective pastor at either extreme. The differences in the two churches' websites say less about the comparative vanity or humility of the pastors than they do about how each community situates its ordained leader as a symbol of its core identity in the context of the church tradition as a whole. As we've seen, these differences are rooted in complex histories and theologies that express themselves in distinct denominational (or, in the case of Harvest Bible Chapel, non-denominational) characters that are presented relatively flatly through media that project into the present without much reference to the past, unless it is offered intentionally, as Wicker Park Lutheran does.

Digital Faith the Size of a Mustard Seed: A Small Advantage

If we change the channel somewhat and visit each church community's Facebook page, the differences in communication styles—and

Figure 5: Harvest Bible Chapel (Elgin) Facebook page

some similarities in awkwardness with new modes of digital social communication—become clearer still. As a social networking platform, Facebook constrains the graphical glitz that often makes more commercial church websites appear more attractive. On Facebook, everyone's page is pale blue on white. Everyone is limited to the same size profile image and the same mode of interaction on the page "Wall," where messages, photos, event listings, and links to content outside of Facebook are posted. There are actually lots of other things that can be done on a Facebook group page. Members can record or post videos, for instance, or add a wide range of games and gadgets. But now that the newness of the Facebook experience has generally worn off, most users stick with the basics: status updates, photos, links, events, and occasional rants about unwanted Farmville requests.

As we see in the screen shots of the respective Facebook walls—generally the home page of an individual or group on Facebook—the Harvest Bible Chapel Elgin campus page [Figure 5] has significantly more members than does the Wicker Park Lutheran

Figure 6: Wicker Park Lutheran Church Facebook page

Church page [Figure 6]. But we have to bear in mind that the Elgin campus boasts four thousand members. The 583 of these who have joined the Facebook group represent about 15 percent of the total attendance. By contrast, Wicker Park Lutheran's seventy-nine Facebook group members represent more than half of its small congregation.

In any case, as we'll recall from the discussion of the "Dunbar Number" in Chapter 6, numbers don't really tell the story, or at least they don't tell it in quite the way the Broadcast Age has led us to believe. In a world dominated by broadcast media, the most effective communications were judged to be those that drew the most eyes to see or ears to hear. To the extent that the goal of an organization is to grow in the number of contacts—if you're selling a product, for instance—this may well still be an effective measure. But it's certainly not the only one, and, perhaps more importantly, it's not one that is particularly valued by participants in the digitally enhanced world.

Facing the Digital Reformation:
How Images Bridge Digital & Local Community

As we have learned, it is not the number of friends or followers a community has but the quality of interactions that matters, and in this regard both Wicker Park Lutheran and Harvest Bible Chapel have a way to go. Still, the Wicker Park page moves more in the direction of the participative communication style that characterizes more effective leadership for community in the Digital Reformation generally. Even in what is clearly a very early stage of the small church's engagement with its community through digital media, its Facebook page presents the whole of the congregation through an array of photographs showing people (and their pets) at services in the church, in community food-sharing ministries, at choir rehearsals, at yoga and tai chi classes, and so on, as well as gatherings of community members at concerts, picnics, ice skating parties, and other social occasions.

These photos do what broadcast media advertisers have long known that images do far better than words: They evoke feelings, they trigger our intuitive sense of the reality we're seeing. The fact that the pictures on the Wicker Park Facebook page are not staged, formal, professional images immediately stirs in someone who looks at them the same sort of responsive warmth and affection that those adorable YouTube videos of puppies frolicking in the grass and baby monkeys playing with kittens evoke in us, no matter how much work we have piled on our desks. We might recall, too, that much of the rich medieval tradition of affective piety is anchored to the emotional effect of images on believers.

Though day-to-day interaction on the church's Facebook wall proper is more limited—as well it might be in a community in which people seem to hang out together quite a lot in face-to-face settings—the conversation around the photos is animated. Folks coo over babies, tease each other, applaud each other's accomplishments, and those who have moved away check in on life in the Wicker Park Lutheran community. In this way, the Facebook page serves as an interactive scrapbook for the church that shows a diversity of congregants engaged in a small but vibrant community. Communication is still initiated mainly from the rector and the page administrator, but it extends through the community in multi-directional, networked conversations.

Wicker Park Lutheran Church's website does not include a link to its Facebook page—a missed opportunity—but a visitor who happened to find the page through a random search (as I did) has the opportunity to experience something of the tone of engagement and interaction of the community. Its Facebook presence takes it meaningfully beyond the "just the facts" presentation of the website. It moves, that is, toward the social rather than the strictly homiletic and informational. In this sense, its social media practice is consistent with the general communication style of mainline Protestantism as this reflects a more distributed, less hierarchical Protestant ecclesiology.

By contrast, the Harvest Bible Chapel Facebook pages tend to highlight the role of pastors in the news and events it posts. The picture that defines the group page identity echoes the church webpage by featuring the image, words, and recorded voice of Pastor MacDonald. In this sense, the page very effectively follows the logic of broadcast communication which insists on a consistency of images and messages across platforms so that a stronger "brand identity" is developed.[2]

Beyond this, photos included on the Harvest Bible Chapel Facebook page, most of them professional quality, highlight the large, theater-style church, which is shown empty in various lighting as well as filled with masses of unidentifiable audience members. People are usually shown from behind as they gather around or listen attentively to the pastor. Only one photo seems to have been posted by someone outside the church staff, this of a posed group shot from a gathering of some sort that is not described in any meaningful way. The pictures are for the most part neither shared memories nor invitations to engagement. This does provoke an emotional response. But it is not a particularly positive one. At best, it is neutral. But at least for members of mainline churches and those who would be attracted to them, images that tend to say "Big. Empty. Anonymous." are less than emotionally engaging.

There's a certain irony here in that it might seem that a Facebook page or Twitter feed that simply posts notices of upcoming events will more effectively draw people to face-to-face worship. If the research by Grace Davie, which we reviewed in Chapter 3, on vicarious religious practice as it develops in relation to broadcast media can be extended into the digital social media domain, there might appear to be some risk in locating social interaction in an online environment. And, if Satoshi Kanazawa's research on friendships projected onto media personalities, which we discussed in Chapter 5, is accurate, we might want to avoid offering photos that invite artificial relationship.

Certainly, some balance is required so that members of online networks develop a level of engagement that reinforces their interpersonal connectedness without inviting a fantasy of participation that makes face-to-face engagement seem redundant. If I can hear the pastor's sermon on a website podcast, and especially if this message of faith is presented as the center of the worship experience, why get out of my jammies on a blustery Chicago morning? If I can hang out with cool people on Facebook, why drag myself even a few blocks from my cozy living room? But when it comes to inviting people into face-to-face engagement—as we've learned through more than a decade of experience with online dating—seeing faces matters.[3] For a generation schooled on slick media manipulation, it matters especially that the faces are of real people engaging with other real people rather than those of professional posed "personalities."

Wicker Park Lutheran Church's Facebook presence avoids encouraging vicarious participation by sharing visual content that invites members to reflect on the social meaning of their engagement in the church community and informational content that invites them to continue that engagement. Visitors to the page who are not part of the community get to see something meaningfully human about the church as a gathered people, but they can only really access the depth of that engagement by actually showing up at a local church gathering. They can see through a diverse album of photos—more than sixty, compared to the dozen in the Harvest Bible Chapel album—people with identifiable faces worshiping, working, celebrating, and generally being the Body of Christ together. It is clear that the church is about these people, and this is its own invitation to participation in a digitally enhanced worshipping community.

The Harvest Bible Chapel page for the Elgin campus takes rather a different tack. For starters, its Facebook group doesn't open to the Facebook wall where leaders and community members might post information, commentary, or photos. Rather, it opens to the "Info" tab, which provides information on the biblical mission of the church, links to four different websites related to the church, and an email address for more information. An attempt at hipness from the local campus pastor ("it's time for the west side to represent") is the single non-corporate message on the page. Posts generally relate to upcoming or recently completed events at the church. One of the posts inadvertently invites people *not* to attend an upcoming event by providing a link to an online streaming site *before* the event takes place. It almost seems as if visitors are *not* meant to interact with each other—as though the Facebook wall were a *barrier between* rather than a *site for* sharing across the congregation. It has a personality, but it's hardly personal.

Tweeting in the Echo Chamber: Broadcast Practices in New Media Spaces

The same pattern is continued in Pastor MacDonald's Twitter feed (*@jamesmacdonald*), which is updated several times a day, far more frequently than is the Facebook page. Here again, MacDonald has a tremendous following, with more than thirteen thousand "followers." He tweets about the family, biblical authority, his various books and speaking engagements, the growth of Harvest Bible Chapel worldwide, snippets of scripture, and so on:

- We must protect, defend, and give our greatest effort for the success and the strength of our families.
- The Bible is not your authority as long as you're picking and choosing the parts you like.
- Heading to Ft. Worth, TX this afternoon to speak at the @true woman conference.
- The 6th Harvest Bible Chapel of Liberia launched this weekend! 14 Harvest churches now outside of North America in five countries.

On Twitter, engagement is often indicated by the degree to which followers "retweet" messages, sharing them with followers on their own Twitter feeds. Most of MacDonald's Twitter followers do not share his tweets with other Twitter members by "retweeting" them. This is reasonably common on Twitter, which tends to be a more commercial, "push" medium, through which messages are sent out to followers rather than being designed to draw followers into the conversation.

MacDonald is a fairly active tweeter, posting about three tweets each day, more toward the weekend.[4] And, his retweet rate is just shy of ten percent, so his message is getting some play. However, his network of retweeters tends to be other Harvest Bible Chapel pastors, other non-denominational leaders, and Christian media celebrities. Most of these are among the seventy-one people whom MacDonald himself follows. That is, he tends to be in a bit of an echo chamber as far as his Twitter interaction is concerned.

Here we see a communication practice of leaders talking with leaders, while followers observe from the sidelines. This approach to social media communications and leadership might work within the non-denominational or Evangelical ecclesiology to the extent that it reinforces the leadership hierarchy that anchors spiritual identity in the church. But such an approach would be unlikely to work within mainline traditions.

@TexasBishop Tweets Medieval: Social Practices for the Digital Reformation

While Reverend VanDemark does not yet use Twitter in the context of her ministry, at least one Episcopal bishop has begun to develop an approach to social media that recalls much of the social reading practice that, as we discussed in Chapter 3, was common in the medieval church. Andy Doyle tweets as "@TexasBishop." With just over four thousand followers, he is hardly as popular as MacDonald. What I see as an important distinction, however, is that Doyle himself follows more than three thousand Twitter friends, the majority of them members of his diocese, but many from across and well outside the Episcopal Church. The balance between people Doyle himself follows on Twitter and those who follow his tweets marks the bishop as attentive to the voices of a wide and diverse community.

Like MacDonald, he averages about three tweets per day, but Doyle "hashtags" all of them with the word "Episcopal," and other themes such as "evangelism," "economy," and "faith." Hashtagging—placing a # before a word—is a practice which makes tweets searchable, so it links Doyle's tweets into a more extensive, potentially global conversation.

Dialogue is central to Doyle's use of social media. His tweets appear both on his Twitter feed and on Facebook so that more people can participate. Beyond this, rather than announcing events, making moral pronouncements, or celebrating church successes, Doyle has developed a Socratic tweeting style that offers thoughts and questions on important issues in the diocese and the church more generally. When I was observing his Twitter feed particularly closely in the fall of 2010, between snippets from Morning and Evening Prayer, links to news reports on issues in the church, and data points from Pew and other religion research sources, Doyle was on a bit of an evangelism kick:

- #Episcopal #evangelism thought: can we imagine a team of five per church who facilitate small group-based ministry in the neighborhood
- #Episcopal #evangelism thought: we need to seek out those who have a peripheral relationship with the church
- #Episcopal #Evangelism thought: we need to realize many "do not belong because of outcomes of previous belonging"
- #Episcopal #evangelism thought: we must form deep relationships with those OUTSIDE our churches

Doyle's evangelism discussion was prompted by his reflections on an article by theologian Sheryl A. Kujawa-Holbrook, "Evangelism and the Under-Thirty Crowd,"[5] and his ongoing interest in developing dialogue through social media. "I wanted to create space for conversation, so I started posting my thoughts on the article," he explains. "I didn't post quotes from the article itself. I gave people links back so they could read it and share their own thinking."

What followed from this social reading experiment was both a level of exchange that enriched Doyle's own reading of the article and a rare opportunity to observe people in his diocese in a pattern of conversation with people outside of the diocese or the Church that more broadly illuminates some of the difficulties mainline churches have in engaging others. Here is Doyle's description of the conversation:

> On average, there would be thirty-three comments on my Facebook page with each post that fed from Twitter. These comments came from all kinds of people—Episcopalians, other Christians, Buddhists, Jews, non-believers. Over the course of the day or so that I was tweeting on the article, I saw a really amazing thing emerge . . . At first, after each tweet, there is an open conversation that goes on among all these different people. But, as soon as it gets a little out of the comfort zone, Episcopalians kind of take over the conversation and try to drive it to a doctrinal place. It gets almost so closed that fellow Episcopalians who agree with them can't get them back to the global conversation. That wider conversation really gets closed down. If you examine it from the lens of what the article was saying—which was that we have no idea how to talk with the wider culture—it was a brilliant enactment of exactly that.

Doyle has used the episode with clergy in the Diocese of Texas as a case study in the communication style of Episcopalians in the diocese (at the very least), the value of new media for encouraging diverse conversation on important issues in the church, and, for leaders in ministry in particular, the significance of digital platforms as venues for active listening and observation. The experience, says Doyle, "helped me to understand how to talk to people about this phenomenon. I've been able to talk with clergy, for instance, about how we need to get really secure about what we believe. Until we do that, it's really hard for us to talk about anything else. So, this whole social media conversation helped me to see some of our impediments in ways that I would never have been able to see. I don't think we'd ever have this kind of opportunity in another format."

At the level of raw data, this more widely participative communication style results in an impressive retweet rate of nearly 15
percent for Doyle, and his tweets are shared by a number of more
influential tweeters who function as "thought leaders"—people
whose interests and perspectives tend to shape the thinking of
others in their networks—in the Episcopal Church and in religion
more generally. He is, to apply the latest jargon in social media,
"discoverable" by lots and lots of people. His Twitter and Facebook following carries these conversations across his diocese and
through the wider church, so the conversations Doyle starts among
folks in his diocese as well as the patterns of communication these
conversations illustrate extend across a much wider constituency.
Any of us who are interested in how people in the church are talking about a particular topic can join in, observe, or both.

Says Doyle of his commitment to social media participation
within the context of his ministry,

> There is just no way this is not a good use of my time as a bishop.
> It's not just that I'm staying in touch with this circle of people who
> are all interested in what each other has to say. It's not just that
> I'm making some connection with a person in India, talking about
> boundaries for Christian mission work, for example. It's that people
> in our diocese, in our churches are getting connected in an interest-
> ing way because I'm doing this social media work. So I am fulfilling
> my role of being "the church," "the connection," among congrega-
> tions and in the wider world for all of the people in my diocese.

Neither Doyle nor the Lutheran remnant gathered in Wicker
Park have much by way of high-end socio-technical wizardry or
big-budget media experience at their disposal. Yet, in their modest
ways, both have begun to reshape the status quo of religious communication that put mainline churches on the sidelines for most of
the twentieth century. Now that the basic tools are more universally
available and usable by ordinary folk whose geekiness is usually
reserved more for spiritual pursuits than technological ones, they've
drawn on a long tradition of invitation, hospitality, participation,
collaboration, and sharing that emerges in the digital domain as a

new opportunity to see each other, if not face-to-face, in ways that are important adjuncts to local, interpersonal relationship.

Communication in this new reality is not what it's been in the church for maybe a couple millennia, and in the context of digital media it significantly changes the practice of leadership. Fortunately, we have exemplars throughout the tradition and role models across the Church today who are marking a path of change that offers hope for all of us as we more actively practice church in the Digital Reformation.

Digital Social Rule of Life (1.0)

Out of the digital habitus that has begun to emerge, some loosely defined "rules" for digital social practice have emerged. I've shared a few of them below, but it's worth taking a look at the popular social media wisdom site *Mashable* periodically for new social media tools and practices to support the development of meaningful connection and enriched community.

To Have a Friend, Be a Friend

As a rule of thumb, it's good to follow at least as many people on Twitter as follow you. It's generally polite to "follow back" people who follow you, unless they're clearly marketers trying to sell you something in which you have no interest. Likewise, it's good digital leadership practice to accept Facebook friend requests from whoever asks—again, unless you can discern a less than friendly motivation. Though this is rarely necessary—I've done it exactly one time in the last four years—if Facebook friends misbehave, you can message them privately, block their posts, and, as a last resort, "unfriend" them entirely.

Keep the Church Doors Open

When I share this advice with churches and leaders in ministry, it almost always raises questions about privacy, especially—and very appropriately—the privacy of those who friend or follow them. Whatever our formal or informal role in the Church, we conduct our ministries in public. The Church is not a secret society, which seems to mean that we really ought to allow anyone access to our digital communities who would have access to our face-to-face communities. "As ministers, we're public people," says Lutheran Pastor Keith Anderson. "We might want to forget that from time to time, but we can't escape it and really be doing what we are called to do."

There are good reasons for having private Facebook groups or limited access Twitter feeds, but very few of them. Clusters of people in online prayer circles or covenant groups, as well as groups or individuals who might be subject to bullying or proselytizing, have reason to limit access. As more online religious education moves to social media platforms, managing access to copyrighted and other proprietary materials will require the development of closed spaces. And there are good pedagogical and formational reasons for setting up smaller online Bible study and similar groups. But I can think of no good reason for limiting access to a broader church-related Facebook page, Twitter feed, or other social media hub—especially when options for private conversations via messaging features on both Facebook and Twitter are available. Or, you can always go old-school and pick up the phone.

Tweet a Simple Melody, Not a Symphony

A Twitter feed can absorb a meaningful tweet every hour or so through the day, more if you're tweeting from an event or within a particular conversation. Most people, however, find getting a string of tweets seconds apart to be a bit much. On Facebook, you have the opportunity to share *slightly* longer posts, which means it takes people more time to read them. Posting long missives—any more than about fifty words—or posting more than every few hours through the day tends to be overkill, especially if you're not attending to what other people are sharing as well.

Share the Love, Honestly

Sharing is at the core of social media practices, making it a central value in the Digital Reformation. It's wonderful, then, to repost or retweet quotes, news stories, blog links, videos, and other cool stuff you come across through your friends and followers. But it's rude not to acknowledge that debt. It undermines relationships, erodes ethical practice, and ultimately weakens community. Be generous, then, in recognizing those who've been generous with you by naming them in your retweets and reposts.

Branching Out

At a certain point—when you're connected to a sufficiently diverse group of people who may know you in different ways—it can be a good idea to have separate spaces online for these, just as you have separate spaces for them in the physical world. Your church or organization should have its own Facebook page and perhaps a Twitter feed where it's appropriate to announce events, post photos, and share other information that is specifically relevant to that context. Many of the friends and followers on your personal pages will also connect to your institutional pages, and you can invite others if you feel that they're missing out on information and connections that would be meaningful to them.

Making the Rules

This short list of tips is just a starting point for reflection on what a new Digital Rule of Life might look like. Indeed, it can be useful to talk with members of your local and digital community about how best to engage digital social media environments in both functional and ethical terms. A few churches and other religious organizations are beginning to develop more formal policies for social media engagement, the thrust of which is generally related to reducing liability. If we recall Dean David Bird's question about such issues from the beginning of the book, the development of very clear policies is almost certainly a good idea. But it's important not to value them over meaningful practices of communication, community, and leadership. Both policies *and* practices, then, should be articulated as clearly as possible in your community and assessed and revised frequently on the basis of day-to-day practice.

IF YOU MEET LUTHER,
CALVIN, OR HOOKER
ON THE ROAD

The wind blows where it chooses, and you hear the sound of it, but you do not know where it comes from or where it goes.

—*John 3:8*

In a well-known Buddhist teaching, the ninth-century master Lin Chi tells followers that they must have no attachments, not even to the Buddha himself. In Buddhist practice, attachment to anything—a person, an object, an idea—is an illusion that keeps one from finding true enlightenment. Thus, he tells his students that if they should come upon the Buddha on the road, they should not bow before him. They should kill him.

It's a hard teaching, but of course Christianity is not without its own hard teachings, most of them offered by the Jesus of the Gospels as he attempts to guide disciples away from attachments that keep them from participating in the Kingdom of God. Jesus tells a disciple to "let the dead bury their own dead" (Matthew 8:22), but not because he lacks compassion for a child who has lost a parent. Neither does he turn away from his mother and brothers (Matthew 12:46–49) because he is "anti-family." And, of course, his promise to destroy the temple (John 2:19) has nothing to do with any disdain for organized religion in general or Judaism in particular.

All of these difficult teachings, like Lin Chi's call for his students to "kill the Buddha," confront rigid attachments to personalities, rituals, institutions, and traditions—elements of the dominant habitus that keep us from living in the Spirit of God's radical love, justice, and abundance. To the extent that we are unable to let go of these attachments, Jesus tells us that we are pretty much dead to the life God gives us in the here and now and to the promise of eternal life in the sweet hereafter. Our only attachment—and here Christians are very different from Buddhists—should be to the God of love, whom we experience in loving relationship with others of all sorts and through whatever we are able to understand as our truest self.

On some level, we all know this story, and we're all aware that we fail everyday to live out what are almost certainly sincere and heartfelt commitments to the Gospel of love, justice, and peace. Like poor St. Paul, we all do that which we would not do (Romans 7:15). In terms of whatever might function as our individual spiritualities, I suppose that's between each of us and our loving, forgiving God. But for the Church as the present incarnation of the Body of Christ, it's a much bigger deal when we hold on to practices that feed our particular souls but which may not nourish the Body as a whole. Keith Anderson describes it this way:

> Sometimes walking into our churches is like going back in time. It's as if nothing's changed in the world for fifty or sixty years except that we don't wear hats anymore. You kind of see that the Church is just not living where people are. A lot of the time, we're like a treasured, valuable antique that we don't want to get rid of, but we can't really use to connect to the world in the way we did in the past.

Anderson is not suggesting that we chuck the whole of Christian or Reformation tradition, and practices that have been the rich foundations of diverse, distinctive, yet nonetheless interdependent communities for generations. But it does seem clear that the tendency of mainline churches to prioritize ministry, evangelism, formation, and witness in the bricks-and-mortar church has allowed these buildings to become anchors, if not outright idols, in the service of God. If we take Jesus at his word, that the Spirit of God "blows where it chooses," we cannot ignore the sound of it—not only in the digital world proper but in the participative, creative, collaborative, and overall improvisational practices emerging from our increasingly digitally integrated lives.

The new digital habitus thus invites a very different practice of church than many people in mainline congregations and many mainline leaders in ministry are used to. But mainline churches don't come into the Digital Reformation quite as mainline as they used to be. For much of the last generation, Evangelical and non-denominational churches were clearly more "mainline" in terms of their political influence and cultural significance. Through the lingering recession that began in 2008, however, membership in Evangelical churches has begun to plateau. The bankruptcy of Robert Schuller's famed Crystal Cathedral and the formation by Schuller's grandson Bobby of a more intimate, "post-boomer" church stand as signs of what many sociologists see as a coming decline in membership after the long Evangelical ascendancy.[1] While the Roman Catholic Church has seen increased membership in parts of Africa and Latin America, the overall trend since the 1960s in North America and Europe has been downward. No Christian denomination seems to be particularly "mainline" anymore.

As I've suggested throughout the book, this would be rather bad news were it not for the fact that it puts the Church much closer to the margins of society again. If we are meant to use the ministries of Jesus, his earliest disciples, and those of any number of outcast mystics, rogue theologians, renegade preachers, and uppity laypeople as examples, this seems to be the locale where we do our best work. And, even if our ministries must now extend beyond the solid, physical spaces where we have traditionally gathered for worship, fellowship, learning, and service, our traditions still have much to offer the Church in the digital world.

Perhaps chief among the lessons our history teaches us is that our traditions have always been both durable and malleable. From the start, Christians have been improvisers and samplers— multi-cultural, multi-millennia, global mash-up artists. Maybe all this technology and the change it is creating seems overwhelming, but at the end of the day, we're people of the Resurrection. We are always born, and born again. Our traditional belief in transformation, then, both calls us to and prepares us for life in this period of profound renewal in the church.

As in the last great Reformations, some of this renewal has to do with roles and authority. "With the advent of a new medium, the status quo not only comes under scrutiny; it is revised and rewritten by those who have gained new access to the tools of its creation," says technology writer Douglas Rushkoff.² We see this rewriting and revision in the numerous prayer pages across the social media landscape and in smartphone apps that enable people to access, interpret, and share passages from scripture, history, and doctrine across digital and physical landscapes with digital and traditional communities of friends. Through the proliferation of religious, spiritual, denominational, and otherwise configured Christian Facebook groups, barriers between local churches and within and across denominations have begun to be eroded.

These developments highlight the new ways in which mainline Christians are ministering to one another more directly already. The "Holy Roller" app that I mentioned in the Introduction was developed by Ryan Dry, a layperson who doesn't really see himself as a "leader" or a "minister" in the church. He makes no claim on the leadership of Christ United Methodist Church outside of Plano, Texas, where he grew up, met his wife, and where their kids were baptized. But, as the app connects believers and their networks when they share on Facebook and Twitter the Bible verses they've "rolled" to address their "blessings" or "burdens," it does express and shape a new kind of leadership and ministry among ordinary believers.

This has profound implications for the definition of pastoral roles, ecclesial authority, and, ultimately, church organization and structure that extend well beyond the digital domain. A whole new improvisational habitus drawn from regular engagements with digital social media throughout our lives threatens to distribute the practice of church into dissolution. At the very same time, it holds out the promise of renewal by reconnecting us to modes of interpersonal relatedness and diverse community that are at the heart of Christian discipleship. Formal and informal leaders in ministry have at this very moment in the history of the Church a remarkable power to tip the balance of that equation one way or the other. They could either opt out of the Digital Reformation and allow the rapid disintegration of institutional religion to continue apace, or they could become engaged and engaging participants whose practices create space for others to grow spiritually in the context of newly revitalized, digitally integrated communities of faith.

Now, as Paul surely understood, as the desert Ammas and Abbas knew, and as other ancient and medieval Christians attempted to minimize through practices of strict obedience, new practices of relatedness are often painfully difficult to undertake. Lining us all up in separate rows and sections like words on the pages of so many new books in the aftermath of the sixteenth-century Reformation has perhaps allowed a necessary respite from long centuries of Christian persecution, dissention, repression, and division. However, what many scholars are calling "the modern parenthesis" is now coming to an end, and we are called again to take up the challenging work of facilitating the balance of Christian unity and diversity that enables us to do God's work in a world of need. Leaders in ministry with sufficient sophistication in social practices that bridge face-to-face and digital environments are, I would argue, at the spiritual and ethical center of this challenge.

Fortunately, we come into this Digital Reformation with a deep reserve of wisdom, the promise of grace, and a storehouse of basic Christian practices that translate easily into new environments. At the most basic level, communication, community, and leadership in the Digital Reformation are most effectively undertaken with practices of listening, attentiveness, connecting, and engaging that have shaped Christianity since Mary overcame her own fear to listen to the angel Gabriel as he shared God's blessing and holy plan for her. Things haven't been the same since.

For leaders in ministry—whatever that comes to mean within the improvisational habitus of the Digital Reformation—applying these practices through digital social media doesn't guarantee that droves of people will be lining up at mainline churches or related organizations anytime soon. As I've said throughout this book, I don't know that "droves" are really the ideal setting for ministry among mainline Christians. Indeed, I'm unconvinced that mass market Christianity is a good idea overall. But if we update practices that have served us reasonably well for some two thousand years, I do believe we will be able to enrich relationships and build communities that will allow us to more generously live out the commitments of our faith. The opportunities for this in the spiritual spaces created by digital social media as they extend into face-to-face relationships and communities are tremendous.

Our challenge is to approach these opportunities not out of fear and anxiety that cause us to cling to our traditions instead of learning from them. Rather, we must embrace the opportunities presented by digital social media out of the same love and hope that names us as Christians, that forms and reforms us again and again as Church. This optimistic embrace, it seems to me, is a much greater challenge than figuring out how to integrate the most vexing new gadget or bustling online locale into our lives. Yet my own engagement with the riches of Christian history and tradition and with the improvisations of so many leaders in ministry in new digital spiritual spaces make me confident that we're up to it.

"Is social media the end of the church, or a new beginning?" a friend wondered one day, as we walked through a neighborhood park.

"Yes," I answered, remembering T. S. Eliot's homage in "Four Quartets" to the new community of prayer and service that Nicholas Ferrar and his extended family created in the English countryside during another period of great change in the church:

> What we call the beginning is often the end
> And to make an end is to make a beginning.
> The end is where we start from. . . .
>
> We shall not cease from exploration
> And the end of all our exploring
> Will be to arrive where we started
> And know the place for the first time. . . .
>
> And all shall be well and
> All manner of thing shall be well. . . .[3]

Notes

Introduction

1. William R. Hutchinson, *Between the Times: The Travail of the Protestant Establishment in America, 1900–1960* (Cambridge and New York: Cambridge University Press, 1990), 6. However, as I note below, Baptists have tended to have more in common with evangelical and non-denominational churches than with the mainline churches which emerged most directly from the Reformation (Anglican/Episcopal, Lutheran, Presbyterian).

2. On this, see Chapter 7.

3. Hua Wang and Barry Wellman, "Social Connectivity in America: Changes in Adult Friendship Network Size from 2002 to 2007," *American Behavioral Scientist*, vol. 53, no. 8 (April 2010): 1148–1169.

4. Janet Thomas, "MP3 Players Offer Sermons in Child Language." *Interpreter Magazine*, *http://www.interpretermagazine.org/interior_print. asp?ptid=43&mid=14239&pagemode=print*. Accessed July 17, 2010; Oliver Moore, "Nova Scotia Priest Plans to Bless the Faithful's [*sic*] Cellphones," *The Globe and Mail*, online edition, *http://tinyurl.com/grace gadgets* (September 1, 2010). Accessed September 2, 2010.

5. The rapid development of apps makes it impossible to give an exact count. In August 2009, for instance, there were about 350 apps related to the Bible. By January 2010, that number had doubled.

6. Search of Facebook and iTunes conducted on July 16, 2010. See also: Paul Vitello, "You Say God is Dead? There's an App for That," *New York Times* (July 2, 2010). Accessed online at *http://www.nytimes. com/2010/07/03/technology/03atheist.html*.

7. *The Budget*, established in Sugarcreek, Ohio in 1890, publishes letters written by Amish and Mennonite "scribes" from communities in Indiana, Ohio, and Pennsylvania, as well as from "Plain People" in Canada and Central and South America. While the national edition is distributed in Amish and Mennonite communities in print format, the local edition is available online at *http://www.thebudgetnewspaper.com*.

8. "In U.S., Increasing Number Have No Religious Identity," Gallup (May 21, 2010). Accessed online at *http://www.gallup.com/poll/128276/Increasing-Number-No-Religious-Identity.aspx*.

9. However, as I note in the Conclusion, the growth trend in Evangelical and non-denominational churches is beginning to stall.

10. Data summary from ARIS 2008 report, 5, correlated to Pew 2008 U.S. Religious Landscape Survey, 102–106.

11. Pew Forum on Religion and Public Life, "U.S. Religious Landscape Survey—Religious Affiliation: Diverse and Dynamic" (February 2008): 31. Accessed online at *http://religions.pewforum.org/pdf/report-religious-landscape-study-full.pdf*.

12. Barry A. Kosmin and Ariela Keysar, "American Religious Identification Survey [ARIS 2008]," Trinity College, Hartford, CT (March 2009). Available online at *http://www.americanreligionsurvey-aris.org/reports/ARIS_Report_2008.pdf*. Pew Forum on Religion & Public Life, "U.S. Religious Landscape Survey—Religious Affiliation: Diverse and Dynamic" (February 2008). See also Barry A. Kosmin, et al., "American Nones: The Profile of the No Religion Population." Trinity College, Hartford, CT (2009). Stewart M. Hoover, et al., "Faith Online." Pew Internet & American Life Project (April 7, 2004) and Elena Larson, "CyberFaith: How Americans Pursue Religion Online." Pew Internet & American Life Project (December 23, 2001). On home internet access rates, see Steve Crabtree, "Countries with High Home Internet Access Span Regions," Gallop (July 28, 2010). Unless otherwise noted, data cited throughout this book come from these studies.

13. Recent examples include: Nicholas Carr, *The Shallows: What the Internet Is Doing to Our Brains* (New York: Norton, 2010) and William Powers, *Hamlet's Blackberry: A Practical Philosophy for Building a Goof Life in the Digital Age* (New York: Harpers, 2010).

14. See, for example, Clay Shirky, *Cognitive Surplus: Creativity and Generosity in a Connected Age* (New York: Penguin, 2010) and Frank Langfitt, "Mobile Money Revolution Aids Kenya's Poor, Economy," National Public Radio (January 6, 2010). Accessed online at *http://www.npr.org/2011/01/05/132679772/mobile-money-revolution-aids-kenyas-poor-economy*.

15. Austin Considine, "And on the Sabbath, the iPhones Shall Rest," *New York Times* (March 17, 2010).

16. *Oxford English Dictionary*, s.v., "communicate," "common."

17. My discussion of "habitus" throughout relies primarily on the work of Pierre Bourdieu, which is detailed in *Outline of a Theory of Practice*, 2nd ed., trans. Richard Nice (Cambridge: Cambridge University Press, 2006).

18. David B. Barrett, George T. Kurian, and Todd M. Johnson, *World Christian Encyclopedia: A Comparative Survey of Churches and Religions in the Modern World*, 2nd ed. (New York: Oxford University Press, 2001).

19. Cited in Emily Jackson, et al., *A History of Hand-Made Lace: Dealing with the Origin of Lace, the Growth of the Great Lace Centres, the Mode of the Manufactures, the Methods of Distinguishing, and the Care of Various Kinds of Lace* (London: Scribner's, 1900).

20. Brenda E. Brasher, *Give Me That Online Religion* (San Francisco: Jossey-Bass, 2001), 32.

Chapter 1

1. Available online at *http://www.youtube.com/watch?v=pQHX-SjgQvQ*.

2. Bourdieu, *Outline of a Theory of Practice*, 124.

3. See Timothy Fry, ed., *The Rule of St. Benedict* (Collegeville, MN: Liturgical Press, 1981).

Chapter 2

1. Bede the Venerable, *The Ecclesiastical History of the English People* (Stillwell, KS: Digireads, 2008), 118.

2. E. Gordon Whatley, ed. and trans., *The Saint of London: The Life and Miracles of St. Erkenwald*. Medieval and Renaissance Text Studies, vol. 58 (Bingham, NY: Center for Medieval and Early Renaissance Text Studies, 1989), 103–109.

3. Mary Cooper, *The Child's New Play Thing: being a Spelling Book Intended To make the Learning to Read a Diversion instead of a Task*, London, 1743. Cited in Ross W. Beals and E. Jennifer Monaghan, "Literacy and Schoolbooks," in Hugh Amory and David D. Hall, eds., *A History of the Book in America*, volume 1, *The Colonial Book in the Atlantic World* (New York: Cambridge University Press, 2000), 3386.

4. However, Douglas Ruskoff argues in *Program or Be Programmed: Ten Commands for the Digital Age* (New York: O/R Books, 2010) that our general inability to understand programming languages and practices prevents us from participating in the structuring of data, knowledge, and meaning that occurs in the development of the technologies we use.

5. Jenifer Johnston, "Teachers Call for Urgent Action as Pupils Write Essays in Text," *The Sunday Herald* (March 2, 2003). Accessed online at *http://findarticles.com/p/articles/mi_qn4156/is_20030302/ai_n12581159*, April 15, 2009.

6. Michael O'Malley, "Cleveland Bishop Seeks Meeting with Breakaway Catholics," Religion News Service (August 17, 2010). Accessed

online *http://pewforum.org/Religion-News/RNS-Cleveland-bishop-seeks-meeting-with-breakaway-Catholics.aspx.*

Chapter 3

1. "Church, TV, and Glee," YouTube Video, *http://www.youtube.com/watch?v=y_GH65KRZZI*, accessed September 25, 2010.

2. Grace Davie, "Vicarious Religion: A Methodological Challenge," in Nancy T. Ammerman, ed., *Everyday Religion: Observing Modern Lives*, 21–37 (Oxford: Oxford University Press, 2007).

3. Frederick J. Furnivall, ed., *The Story of England by Robert Manning of Brunne, A.D. 1338*, Rolls Series, No. 87 (London: Longman & Co., 1887), part I, ll. 75–75.

4. Margery Kempe, *The Book of Margery Kempe*, ed. Sanford Brown Meech with an introduction and notes by Hope Emily Allen, vol. 1, (London: Oxford University Press; H. Milford, 1940), 144.

5. Elizabeth L. Eisenstein, *The Printing Press as Agent of Change: Communications and Cultural Transformation in Early Modern Europe*, 2nd ed. (Cambridge: Cambridge University Press, 1994), 131.

6. Grace Davie, *Religion in Britain Since 1945: Believing Without Belonging* (Oxford: Blackwell, 1994), 113.

7. Clifford Peterson, ed., *St. Erkenwald* (Philadelphia: University of Pennsylvania Press, 1977).

8. For "Father Matthew Presents," see *http://www.youtube.com/watch?v=FznbwmCmTOQ*. For Betty Butterfield, see, for example, *http://www.youtube.com/watch?v=OlKpPOTZ_0k*.

Chapter 4

1. Lisa Gitelman, *Always Already New: Media, History, and the Data of Culture* (Cambridge: MIT Press, 2006), accessed via Kindle.

2. Mary E. Hess, "Shaping Spirituality in Web 2.0 Pedagogics: Communicative Theological Practice and Learning in Social Media," paper presented to the Society for the Study of Christian Spirituality at the Annual Meeting of the American Academy of Religion, Atlanta, GA, October 30, 2010.

3. Michael J. Gorman, *Apostle of the Crucified Lord: A Theological Introduction to Paul and His Letters* (Grand Rapids: Eerdmans, 2004), 82.

4. See Dwight J. Freisen, *Thy Kingdom Connected: What the Church Can Learn from Facebook, the Internet, and Other Networks* (Grand Rapids: Baker Books, 2009).

5. Jerome Murphy-O'Connor, *Paul the Letter-Writer: His World, Options, and Skills*, vol. 41 of Good News Studies (Collegeville, MN: Liturgical Press, 1995), 126.

6. Hartford Institute for Religion Research (June 2009), available online at *http://hirr.hartsem.edu/research/fastfacts/fast_facts.html#sizecong*. Accessed August 19, 2009.

Chapter 5

1. Marshall McLuhan and Quentin Fiore, *The Medium Is the Massage: An Inventory of Effects*, 2nd ed. (Berkeley: Ginko Press, 2001).

2. Anselm, *Proslogion: With Replies of Gaunilo and Anselm*, trans. with introduction and notes by Thomas Williams (Indianapolis: Hackett, 2001), vii.

3. Marshall McLuhan, *The Gutenberg Galaxy: The Making of Typographic Man* (Toronto: University of Toronto Press, 1962), 67–70.

4. Robert Bellah, *Beyond Belief: Essays on Religion in a Post-Traditional World*, 2nd ed. (Berkeley and Los Angeles: University of California Press, 1991), 175.

5. *Middle English Dictionary*, s.v. "onen." Accessed online at *http://quod.lib.umich.edu/cgi/m/mec/med-idx?type=idandid=MED30590*.

6. Satoshi Kanazawa, "Bowling with Our Imaginary Friends," *Evolution and Human Behavior*, vol. 23 (2002): 167–171.

7. "Primates on Facebook: Even Online, the Neocortex Is the Limit," *The Economist* (February 26, 2009). Accessed online at *http://www.economist.com/node/13176775?story_id=13176775*, March 18, 2010.

8. Aleks Krotoski, "Robin Dunbar: We Can Only Ever Have 150 Friends at Most," *Guardian* (March 14, 2010), accessed online at *http://www.guardian.co.uk/technology/2010/mar/14/my-bright-idea-robin-dunbar*, March 16, 2010.

9. See, for example, Claire Cain Miller, "Start-Up Plans a More Personal Social Network," *The New York Times* (November 15, 2010) and "Facebook Alternative Diaspora Goes Live," BBC Mobile News (November 24, 2010). Accessed online at *http://www.bbc.co.uk/news/technology-11828245*.

10. Stefana Broadbent, "How the Internet Enables Intimacy," TED Talk (July 2009). Accessed online at *http://www.ted.com/talks/stefana_broadbent_how_the_internet_enables_intimacy.html*.

11. Cynthia M. Baker, *Rebuilding the House of Israel: Architectures of Gender in Jewish Antiquity* (Stanford, CA: Stanford University Press, 2002), 45–46.

12. Walter Ong, *Orality and Literacy: The Technologizing of the World*, 2nd ed. (New York: Routledge, 2002), 133–134.

13. Ibid., 133–134.

14. Rushkoff, *Program or Be Programmed*.

15. Quentin J. Schultze and Robert Woods Jr., *Understanding Evangelical Media: The Changing Face of Christian Communication* (Downers Grove, IL: InterVarsity Press, 2008), 283–284.

16. McLuhan and Fiore, *The Medium Is the Massage*, 81.

Chapter 6

1. Jacques Derrida, "The Almost Nothing of the Unpresentatble," in *Points . . . : Interviews, 1974–1994*, ed. Elisabeth Weber, trans. Peggy Kamuf and others (Stanford: Stanford University Press, 1995), 87.

2. Liston Pope, *The Kingdom Beyond Caste* (New York: Friendship Press, 1957), 31.

3. Ralph Waldo Emerson, "Circles," in *The Essays of Ralph Waldo Emerson*, ed. Alfred Riggs Ferguson and Jean Ferguson Carr (Cambridge: Belnap Press, 1987), 117.

4. Malcolm Gladwell, "Small Change: Why the Revolution Will Not Be Tweeted," *The New Yorker* (October 4, 2010), accessed online at *http://www.newyorker.com/reporting/2010/10/04/101004fa_fact_gladwell*.

Chapter 7

1. Pope Benedict XVI, "The Priest and Pastoral Ministry in a Digital World: New Media at the Service of the World" (May 16, 2010). Accessed online at *http://tinyurl.com/ya2l8b9*.

2. Bottom-up authority is at the heart of theories of social, political, and ecclesial emergence. On this, see Steven Johnson, *Emergence: The Connected Lives of Ants, Brains, Cities, and Software* (New York: Scribner, 2001) and Clay Shirky, *Here Comes Everybody: The Power of Organizing without Organizations* (New York: Penguin, 2008).

3. See, for example, Ken Blanchard and Phil Hodges, *Lead Like Jesus: Lessons from the Greatest Leadership Role Model of All Time* (Nashville: Thomas Nelson, 2005) and Laurie Beth Jones, *Jesus CEO: Using Ancient Wisdom for Visionary Leadership* (New York: Hyperion, 1995), which I would compare to recent work by Margaret Benefiel and N. Graham Standish that takes less commercial and corporate approaches to the spirituality of leadership.

4. "Church Marketing Sucks" (*http://www.churchmarketingsucks.com/*) is a project of the non-profit Center for Church Communications, which provides resources to help churches communicate more effectively through contemporary media.

5. Carter Lindberg, *The European Reformations*, 2nd ed. (Oxford: Blackwell, 2004), 155.

6. Martin Luther, "To the Christian Nobility," in John Dillenberger, ed., *Martin Luther: Selections from His Writings* (New York: Anchor Books, 1962) 407.

7. "The Polity of the Episcopal Church," online presentation available at *http://www.slideshare.net/RSGracey/introduction-to-the-polity-of-the-episcopal-church-part-1* (2008; accessed April 11, 2010).

8. Carl R. Trueman, "Reformers, Puritans and Evangelicals," Chapter 2 of *The Rise of the Laity in Evangelical Protestantism*, ed. Deryck W. Lovegrove (London: Routledge, 2002), 29, n. 27.

9. Schultze and Woods, *Understanding Evangelical Media*, 284.

Chapter 8

1. "Blogging God: On Faith at *www.WashingtonPost.com*," panel discussion at the Annual Meeting of the American Academy of Religion, Atlanta, GA, November 1, 2010.

2. Douglas Burton-Christie, *The Word in the Desert: Scripture and The Quest for Holiness in Early Christian Monasticism* (Oxford and New York: Oxford University Press, 1993), 77.

3. Benedicta Ward, trans., *The Sayings of the Desert Fathers; The Alphabetical Collection* (Kalamazoo, MI: Cistercian Publications, 1975, 1984 revised edition), 145.

4. Laura Swann, *The Forgotten Desert Mothers: Sayings, Lives, and Stories of Early Christian Women* (Mahwah, NJ: Paulist Press, 2001), 35.

5. Ibid., 60.

6. John Chrysostom, *De compunctione ad Stelechium* 2.3, in Claudia Rapp, *Holy Bishops in Late Antiquity: The Nature of Christian Leadership in an Age of Transition* (Berkeley and Los Angeles: University of California Press, 2005), 119,

7. "Social Networks/Blogs Now Account for One in Every Four and a Half Minutes Online," *Neilson Wire* (June 15, 2010). Accessed online at *http://blog.nielsen.com/nielsenwire/global/social-media-accounts-for-22-percent-of-time-online/*.

8. Ben Parr, "Facebook Is the Web's Ultimate Time Sink," *Mashable* (February 10, 2010). Accessed online at *http://mashable.com/2010/02/16/facebook-nielsen-stats/*.

9. See Gary Wolf, "How the Internet Invented Howard Dean," *Wired*, vol. 12, no. 1 (January 2004), accessed online at *http://www.wired.com/wired/archive/12.01/dean.html?pg=1andtopic=andtopic_set=* and David Carr, "How Barack Obama Tapped into Social Networks' Power," *New*

York Times (November 9, 2004). Accessed online at *http://www.nytimes. com/2008/11/10/business/media/10carr.html.*

Chapter 9

1. I conducted a brief telephone interview with the Reverend VanDemark, but was unable to reach either the Reverend MacDonald or the communications staff at Harvest Bible Chapel.

2. On this, see Naomi Klein, *No Logo: No Space, No Choice, No Jobs*, 2nd ed. (New York: Picador, 2009), which discusses the impact of corporate branding on culture, identity, and community.

3. Judith Donath and danah boyd, "Public Displays of Connection," *BT Technology Journal*, vol. 22, no. 4 (October 2004): 71–82.

4. Twitter analytics from TweetStats (*tweetstats.com/status/jamesmacdonald*) and Twitalyzer (*http://www.twitalyzer.com/profile.asp?u=jamesmacdonald*). Accessed September 8, 2010.

5. Available online from the Alban Institute at *http://www.alban.org/ conversation.aspx?id=9141.*

Conclusion

1. Steven Church, "Crystal Cathedral Ministries Seeks Bankruptcy, Blames Recession," *The Washington Post* (October 19, 2010). Accessed online at *http://www.washingtonpost.com/wp-dyn/content/article/2010/ 10/19/AR2010101900014.html?hpid=moreheadlines.* Nicole Santa Cruz, "The Schullers: A Tale of Two Churches," *Los Angeles Times* (November 27, 2010). Accessed online at *http://www.latimes.com/news/local/la-me-schuller-family-20101127,0,4079384.story.*

2. Rushkoff, *Program or Be Programmed*, 12.

3. T. S. Eliot, "Little Gidding," in *Four Quartets* (Orlando: Harcourt, 1943, 1971).